GET PUMPED!

Winning with God's Promises

by Coach Joey Hawkins

*This Book Is Dedicated
to My Wonderful Family,
Kim, Hunter, and Holly*

The Hawkins Family

Acknowledgements

I have enjoyed spending time writing my first book. I would like to thank my lovely wife, Kim, for supporting me. Kim you have made me a better person, and you keep me on the right path daily. To my wonderful children Hunter and Holly, you are the greatest gifts in the world, and I love you. I am so thankful to have the best parents, Joe and Sherry, thank you for always being there for me. I would also like to thank all of my friends who have encouraged me, through the years. I have to give a shout-out to my friend Joe McSwain for helping me with this book. I praise the Lord above all for saving me, and giving me strength to serve Him on a daily basis. Thank you, God for loving me, forgiving me, and using me to encourage others.

Joey Hawkins

My Story

I wanted to tell you a little about my life and how the Lord encouraged me to write my first book. I retired from coaching in May of 2018. I have been writing since last March, and I have enjoyed recording on paper, what the Lord has put on my heart. I got saved in April of 1968 in my hometown of Indianola, MS. The Lord blessed me through my high school days and I had a great time playing sports. During my college years, I knew the Lord wanted me to shine for Him. However, I gradually strayed away from the Lord, not a very wise decision. The enemy will lie to you and tell you, "try the world it will make you happy". The Bible says the pleasures of sin are only for a season. This is so true, Satan wants to destroy our relationship with Christ. But thank God for His Amazing Grace that covers all our sins. After drifting in and out of fellowship for nine long years, I returned to the Lord in August of 1988. I asked the Lord to forgive me and show me His plan for my life. Over the next year, I read the Bible four to six hours a day. The Holy Spirit helped me memorize an amazing amount of scripture to encourage others. This is why I wrote this book, to lift someone's spirit and tell them "you can make it" when you call on the Lord.

All of God's promises are for every believer, and God watches over His Word to perform it in your life. Through good times and bad times, Jesus has been my friend for over 50 years. Through many mistakes, the Lord has never given up on me. The Lord will forgive you instantly when you confess your sins, and he will remember them no more. God has blessed me with an awesome family. He also blessed me with a rewarding career as a high school football and track coach for many years. Over my thirty-seven-year coaching career, I served at five outstanding schools and was blessed to coach a great number of outstanding athletes and young men. I had the pleasure to play and coach on a number of championship teams. I pray the words in this book will inspire and encourage you. I also pray that you will become closer to the Lord by reading this book. What a blessing to share the words that the Lord has put on my heart on a daily basis. My heart's desire, is to bless you and give all the glory to God.

Joey Hawkins

- This world is getting so crazy, there is chaos and confusion everywhere you go. But I found a strong tower, a refuge, who will take care of you 24-7! The Lord will give you strength when you are up or down! He will never leave you or forsake you! Hebrews 13:5 He will put your feet on solid ground, and make all your paths straight! Proverbs 3:5-6 He will give you perfect peace in the middle of a storm! Isaiah 26:3 You just keep walking in Love! He will supply every need! Phil.4:19 Nobody like Jesus! Coach

- Some of you have been praying for a long time for the Lord to intervene in your life. I want you to know-He may not come when you want Him- But Jesus is always on time! He fed 5,000 with 2 fish- He healed a blind man with 2 mud pies-He empowered a teenager with acne to kill the biggest Giant in the world-He walked on water-He healed a man that laid by a pool for 38 years-He healed a lady, who tried everything for 12 years, Mark 5:34 Jesus will do it for You!! I would honor Him tonight & call on Jesus! Coach

- There is something about standing on the promises of God and keeping them in front of you, that will cause the Lord to pass over a million people to get to you! 2 Chronicles 16:9 You see, God loves everyone, but you can't please Him without Faith! Hebrews 11:6 Anything you believe in the Bible, will become reality in your life! Mark 11:24 I want you to know Jesus is working all things out for your good tonight! Romans 8:28 Trust Him! Coach

- Have you felt angry, frustrated, and exhausted lately? Well, if you watch the news long enough you can certainly end up in that condition. Satan loves to attack your mental well-being and your physical strength, so that you are just surviving, instead of living more abundantly! John 10:10 The Lord promises He will Refresh the weary and Replenish all who are weak! Jeremiah 31:25 I will give you one more table spoon of medicine, memorize Isaiah 40:31 And you will be on the road to a speedy recovery! Coach

- When you get saved by faith, it is a gift from God. Ephesians 2:8 But once you are born again, living by faith is all up to you! Because faith only comes (one way) by hearing the Word! Romans 10:17 He said, If you abide in Me, and My words in you, you shall ask whatever you desire, and it shall be done to you! John 15:7 He also says, you shall ask anything in My name, I will do it for you! John 14:14 Traditions of men will explain away these verses, but God meant what He said, and said what He meant! They will work 24 hours a day! Praise Him! Leave the results to God! Coach

- Did you know that God has given you the power to never worry again? I mean forever! Oh yes, it is in His Word! He says: Do not be anxious about anything, but in every situation, by prayer & petition, with THANKSGIVING, present your request to God! Phil 4:6 It is impossible to have stress in your life if you are thankful! Cast all your cares on Him, for He cares about you! 1 Peter 5:7 God says: Never worry again! I got this! Coach

- In my 20's I ran away from the Lord. Something I am not proud of at all. But I called on Jesus in August of 1988- and He took me back and put His arms around me and told me, I Love You! In a few weeks, He had me sharing the Gospel everywhere I went! Quit listening to Satan's lies- You are totally qualified to share Jesus! We all have failed and gone astray. Isaiah 53:6 Each day gets sweeter with Jesus! He has brought me out of storms, trials, and dry seasons! I have to praise Him daily! Stay close to Him this year- It will be the greatest decision you have ever made! Coach

- You may have a situation where all the odds are stacked against you, and every voice is saying to accept it. God says: Is there any limit to My Power? I made the heavens and earth with My great Power and My outstretched hand! Nothing is too difficult for Me! Jeremiah 32:17 God loves you & is so eager to help you! Psalms 54:4 God promises He will restore everything you lost and show compassion on you and make you stronger than ever! Deuteronomy 30:3 Read it yourself! God will do it! Coach

- The time will come that you will need faith, either for yourself, or for some member of your family. Faith comes by hearing the Word of God! Romans 10:17 And if you haven't been in your Bible, you will be at a sizable disadvantage when the storms of life come! Get the Word of God, God's Medicine, into your spirit! Proverbs 4:22 And you will defeat giants and see the impossible happen all the time! Matt.17:20 Walking with God is agreeing with His Word! God will not break one promise! Never-Ever-Never! 1 Kings 8:56 & 2 Cor. 1:20 Dust off your Bible and read it! Coach

- God is able to turn your life around in an instant! God is the Father of mercies and the God of all comfort! 2 Cor. 1:2 Just when you think your situation is hopeless, Jesus will send an answer from above! Psalms 116:1 God will give you hope when you are hopeless! God will give you power when you are powerless! God will give you strength, when all of yours is gone! I'm 59 years old, the Lord has never failed me yet! Coach

- Jesus died so we could have an everlasting life! He is going to crack the sky soon and come get His children! Come on now, this is all that matters! We got work to do! We must keep praying and sharing to everyone about what Jesus has done for us! The Lord doesn't want one person to go to hell! 2 Peters 3:9 But the Bible says, that everyone who ever lived on this earth will see Him face-to-face one day! And each one of us will give an account of ourselves to God! Romans 14:11-12 Get filled with the Holy Spirit Tonight!! All you have to do is ask!! Matthew 7:7-11 Coach

- Dwelling on the past, hinders our full participation in the future. Don't let past failures hold you back! We all have been in the same boat! All you have to do is confess your sins, and Jesus is faithful and just to forgive you instantly! 1 John 1:9 Once you ask the Lord to forgive you- you become whiter than snow! Dust yourself off-and get back on your horse, and let's keep telling people there is only one way to Heaven-JESUS!! John 14:6 He shed His blood on that old rugged cross for you! Praise Him! Coach

- You can't walk in the Spirit, and be a gossiper, complainer, and a fault finder of others! The Bible clearly states: Do not judge or you too will be judged! Matthew 7:1 We all have made many mistakes and come short of the glory of God! Romans 3:23 This year let us make up our mind, to uplift, encourage, and see the best in others! Ephesians 4:29-32 And Your days will be filled with joy & laughter as we serve the Lord on a daily basis! Coach

- When you believe and act on a verse in the Bible, you will receive more Power and Strength to win any battle in your life! It only takes one verse to get you saved! John 3:16 Only takes one verse to set you free! John 8:31-32 Only takes one verse to move any mountain in your life! Mark 11:23 Only takes one verse to get you healed! Exodus 23:25 God watches over His Word to perform it 24 hours a day! Jeremiah 1:12 ONLY BELIEVE! Mark 5:36 Coach

- If you are reading this, on the first day of January, I want to give you some good news! You are still here-You are still standing-You Survived-Your still Alive! I know some of you have been through a terrible time. Raise your hands and thank the Lord- His grace & goodness has sustained You! His mercies are new every morning! Lamentations 3:23 Jesus is waiting with open arms tonight to give you rest! Matthew 11:28-30 You run to Jesus this time! He is going to give you a New Start! Coach

- When I was young, "I can do all things" was my favorite verse! Phil. 4:13 But now as I get older, my favorite verse is," Brothers and Sisters, I have not arrived yet, but every day I do ONE THING: I forget the past and look forward to what lies ahead! I press on toward the goal to win the prize of God's heavenly calling in Christ Jesus"! Phil.3:13-14 Coach

- Here are 3 of God's promises just for you! Ask the Lord to bless your plans, and you will be successful in all you do! Proverbs 16:3 Delight yourself in the Lord and He will give you the desires of your heart! Psalms 37:4 Cast your burdens on the Lord, and He will sustain you & uphold you! Psalms 55:22 God's Word is settled in heaven forever! Psalms 119:89 God is Great & Greatly to be Praised! Coach

- Some of your days may have been weary and some of your nights may have been lonely. I am here to tell you- You can wipe away your tears from your eyes. Because God is on your side! Romans 8:31 He can handle anything you are going through! Look Up-Help is on the way! Psalms 121:1-2 You are going to make it! The storm is passing over! God is on your Side! Coach

- Jesus really wants to make you whole. He really desires to be your best friend! He gave His life for you! Have faith in Him-Trust Him with all your heart! You may have to walk 7 times around the wall (Joshua 6:15) or take 7 dips in the river (2 Kings 5:14)-But don't lose hope your Breakthrough is just around the corner! Coach

- On Christmas Day, I have no doubt: Jesus was born in a manger-He died on a cross for our sins-He loves us more than we will ever know-He will deliver us any time we call His Name-He will make a way for us no matter how dark it gets-He will never leave us-and if we put the Word of God first in our lives, He will Heal us-Because the Bible says so! Proverbs 4:20-22 Coach

- You may know some people that wish you would drop dead. They love to see you fail and talk behind your back. But I am here to tell you, on the Eve of Jesus birth, no weapon formed against you will prosper! Isaiah 54:17 Let the haters hate- You are a child of the KING! God has His hand on you! From this day forth, you will be immovable, unshakable, and a blessing to others! The devil tried to destroy you-Why is he running away in stark terror? James 4:7 Because You called on Jesus! The Savior of the world! Merry Christmas! Coach

- When Mary was told that she would conceive of the Holy Spirit and bring forth a son, she could not understand how such a thing could be. In the natural it was impossible. Mary gave us the secret of finding favor with God when she said, " Be it done to me according to your Word (Luke 1:34-38) The natural mind will explain away God's Word. Do like Mary and say: Be it done to me according to your Word, then act accordingly, and it will come to pass! Jesus is the Living Word! John 1:14 Coach

- If we will just trust in the Lord, His ways are so much higher than our ways! He will take you to places you can't imagine!! Isaiah 55 He didn't promise us smooth sailing but always a safe landing! Don't sweat the small stuff! Coach

- It may seem like you are losing in life. I want to give you some good news, if you are holding on to the Word of God- You Will Win! You can do all things through Christ! Phil.4:13 Everything you put your hand to is going to prosper! Psalms 1:3 You are more than a conqueror in Christ! Romans 8:37 Encourage Yourself, with God you are Unbeatable! Coach

- I want to give you Jesus phone number-it is Jeremiah 33:3 Call Him Up! He doesn't have voice mail, He always answers! He will tell you (and even show you) great and mighty things which you do not know! He will also pour His Spirit out on you! Joel 2:28 If your back is up against the wall, Call Him Up! Coach

- One of the greatest things the Lord has ever taught me- is to find a verse in the Bible to cover my case! When you align yourself with God's Promises- All things are possible! Phil. 4:13 If you don't have a verse to fight the enemy- you will always be unsure of God's will in that situation. But when you open the Bible, a shining light will guide you to God's Perfect Will! Psalms 119:105,130 God will always Honor His promises, if we believe! Mark 9:23 Coach

- God created us so we could have an extraordinary relationship with Him! Jesus loves us no matter how many times we have failed Him! There is no sin we have done, that Jesus will not wash away whiter than snow instantly! 1 John 1:9 Christmas time is here- it is time to Praise Him with our whole heart! Hebrews 13:15 It is time to Celebrate Jesus! Love you all. Coach

- Has someone hurt you, talked behind your back, or even left you in a lot of pain! Revenge is of the world-God promises He will fight your battles for you! Exodus 14:14 Don't let someone steal your joy, that Jesus paid for on the cross! Let God's love keep shining through you! Romans 5:5 God's power in you will dominate the devil's plans! Luke 10:19 Keep Smiling! Coach

- If you are in a major storm in your life- I want you to know Jesus is with you! He will make your jagged edges smooth and make your pathways straight! Proverbs 3:5-6 Don't give up, get back up, and fight like you are the 3rd monkey trying to get on Noah's Ark! 1 Timothy 6:12 Coach

- I have no doubt things are going to get better for you! You are going to bounce back and be a blessing to others! Your setbacks have made you seek the Lord- your tough times have made you look for His help! Do like the man did in Mark 1:40-42! He will make you whole! There is Nobody like Jesus! Coach

- Faith in God's Word will help you conquer your problems! It will either create the solution or dominate the situation! The Bible will always give you victory! Make a decision to spend time in God's Word and your life will never be the same! His Blessings will chase you down! Psalms 107:20 Coach

- Don't let anyone, or your traditions, place God in a box! The Bible says: He does great things too marvelous to understand! He performs countless miracles! Job 5:9 He full fills the desires of those who fear Him; He hears their cry and saves them! Psalms 145:19 Call on Him tonight! You will be amazed! Coach

- Faith takes God at His Word! Faith knows that God cannot lie, so faith never argues; but takes it for granted when a request has been made according to the Word of God! Faith considers a work as finished, even before it is manifested! The impossible happens when you believe God's promises! James 1:6-7 Hebrews 11:1,6 Romans 10:17 Coach

- Quit seeking public approval! Jesus was talked about negatively everywhere He went. He just kept doing the will of His Father. Don't lose heart, keep on striving to do the Lord's will. Your most bountiful blessings are just around the corner! Everything you put your hand to, is going to prosper! Deuteronomy 28:1-14 Coach

- Truth always supersedes facts! John 8:31-32 You may have had a really tough time. I mean a season where you were hurt so bad! It was so hurtful, you didn't know if you could make it! But I have some good news for you tonight! The Bible says: Truly I tell you, whatever you ask for in prayer, believe you have received it, and it will be yours! Mark 11:24 This verse has worked for me over and over! Coach

- You were not designed to live in anxiety or under pressure.Phil.4:6 You were made in God's image to bless everyone you come in contact with! Cast all your cares on Jesus because He cares for you! 1 Peter 5:7 Praise the Name of Jesus! Coach

- December can bring happiness in our lives! Whether your 2 or 92, there is something special about Christmas! All kinds of memories, emotions, and sad times & great times happen during this month! But I want to tell you tonight, Jesus was born, He lived for 33.5 years on this earth, and He died for our sins, and He is still alive, and He wants everyone to go to Heaven! And He is so eager to Help you & Heal you in any area of your life tonight! Do not be afraid any longer, ONLY BELIEVE! Mark 5:36 Coach

- Joy is a fruit of the Spirit! One of the greatest gifts from God is Joy! The Bible says: The Joy of the Lord is our strength! Nehemiah 8:10 Don't let anyone or anything ever steal your Joy! Jesus beat the devil on the cross! We are forgiven, and Set Free, and we are going to live in heaven forever! Smile Big and Laugh every day until your ribs hurt! Make the devil mad! Coach

- What do you need tonight? You can try anything or look to anybody to meet your needs. But there is only one person that can meet your needs and His Name is Jesus! He will give you power to make it! He will give you joy unspeakable! He will help you laugh in the middle of a storm! He will give you an abundant & everlasting Life! John 10:10 Your Best Days Are Ahead! Coach

- Satan's # 1 goal: is to make sure we do not read the Bible! You see, the Word brings the perfect will of God. God into every situation! It will bring light into our dark times! Psalms 119:30 The Holy Spirit will give you total victory: no matter what you are going through if you believe the Bible! One verse is all you need! Dust off your Bible tonight & open it up! John 8:31-32 Coach

- Jesus is still the same yesterday, today, and forever. Hebrews 13:8 Whatever He did for others in Matthew-Mark- Luke & John, He will do for you right now! He came to destroy the works of Satan! 1 John 3:8 He will clean up any mess you have made! Call on Him! Coach

- 4 Things that God says if we do: Will give us total healing in our life! It is found in Proverbs 4:20-22
  1) Read your Bible each day! John 1:1
  2) Listen to My Word! Romans 10:17
  3) Keep your eyes on My Word! Psalms 119:11
  4) Meditate on My Word! Joshua 1:8
  Jesus will heal you if you trust Him! Every time! Acts 10:38 Coach

- The greatest place you can be in as a Christian, is standing on the promises of God! Because God is watching over His Word to perform it every day! Jeremiah 1:12 He is looking for His children to believe it! And once you do- Jesus will say to you: Your Faith has made you whole! Mark 5:34 There is only one way to let Jesus be Jesus in your life! And that is believing His Word! Coach

- Jesus has been so good to me! He is my best friend! But there is one verse, that keeps me so motivated to share His Love every day! The Bible says that everyone that ever lived will see Him face to face one day! I don't want anyone to hear these words: I never knew you, Depart from Me. Matthew 7:23 All you have to do, Is say Jesus I believe in you- I believe you died for my sins-forgive me!! And you go to heaven forever! John 3:16 Coach

- Sometimes it seems like the Lord is so far from me. Chaos & confusion starts to creep into my mind and heart. That is when, I start looking back over my life and reflecting on how many times, Jesus has brought me through! He has never failed me yet! Then I say to myself: I can do all things thru Christ- My God shall supply all my needs- He will never leave me or forsake me- He will do exceedingly & abundantly more than I could ever ask or think! I get back up and keep on pressing on with a smile! Coach

- Job was doing well & Satan came in and gave him leprosy from head to toe. Job attended his 10 children's funeral- they all died on the same day. Everyone in town started to despise him. He could have given up, lost his mind, or even committed suicide! But he kept seeking the Lord- and he got double for his trouble! He got blessed beyond measure! He Lived to see his great- great- grand kids! Whatever you have been through- Hold on- Your blessing is on the way! Job 42:10-17 Coach

- Brothers & Sisters it is not the end; it is just the beginning! You may have cried a river, but the Lord is a very present help in time of trouble! Psalms 46:1 You may have had many dark nights, but JOY comes in the morning! Say out loud: I am Back and Better than ever! Jesus will always see you through! Hebrews 13:5 Raise your hands & praise Him! Coach

- Satan is telling some of you:" It is all over, you are a total failure". Don't listen to him, he is a liar! Jesus is saying to you: "It is only just begun, I am starting a new chapter in your life. Do not fear, for I am with you; do not be dismayed, for I am your God. I will strengthen you and help you; I will uphold you with My righteous right hand"! Isaiah 41:10 Coach

- If you make the Lord your refuge, if you make God your shelter, no evil will conquer you, no plague will come near your home! Psalms 91:9-10 I am going to share one more verse today. He says: He will take sickness away from your midst! Exodus 23:25 God is great and greatly to be praised every day! Coach

- Persistence is the key to run this race for Christ! It is bold and daring! Persistence does not look back over its shoulder at yesterday's mistakes! It could care less about public opinion. Persistence holds on to God's promises until they become reality in their life! Psalms 107:20 Coach

- If you feel dismayed, and feel like giving up. Rise up and square your shoulders and say "I will never quit" The Lord has taken me this far, He will never let me down! I have been through some tough times but my best days are ahead! I serve a Mighty God! I am going to thank Him every day! Coach

- In view of what Heaven has for us, run the race with endurance. Be an overcomer and fight back! The prize is greater than the burden! We owe it to God to finish our race for the glory of God! Put on the armor of God and let's roll! Ephesians 6:10-17 Coach

- The Lord is sunshine on a cloudy day! I ran away from Him for 9 years! The Devil thought He had me down for the last count-All hope was gone! But I called on Jesus- and He restored me and made me whole! If you happened to see me crying- I'm doing just fine! Because when I think of all the things Jesus has done for me, I get a little emotional! Coach

- Delight yourself in the Lord and He will give you every desire of your heart! Psalms 37:4 Seek the Lord today, and you will Be on your way to success in all you do! Coach

- Faith in God can help you accomplish anything! Mark 11:22-24 If you have been down and out, call on Jesus today! He will put passion, enthusiasm, and your dreams back into your heart! If you are not spending time with Jesus, you are definitely going the wrong way. Come back to Jesus, He wants to take care of all your troubles, today! Coach

- Rejoice always, pray continually, give thanks in all circumstances, for this is God's will for you through Christ Jesus! 1 Thessalonians 5:16-18 Doing these 3 things each day, will make you have total victory in your life! Coach

- The Bible says, The Power of Life and death, is in the tongue. Proverbs 18:21 Words are containers, they can bring love and encouragement or hurt and pain, instantly to someone! From this day forth; ask the Holy Spirit to help you to discover the value of your words and you will calm storms like Jesus did! Speak life over your family and friends today and you will honor the Lord! Coach

- There are no limits with God. Stop putting a ceiling on what God can do in your life. He has new mercies for you every morning! He fed 5,000 people with 2 fish! He can make a way for you, out of no way! Trust the Lord today and He will bring you out of darkness and into the light! Coach

- God has already given you permission to succeed! It is God's will for you to overcome every obstacle and prosper in spite of your setbacks! 3 John 2 Also no weapon formed against you will prosper! Isaiah 54:17 And the Lord will heal all of your diseases! Psalms 103:3 These are fabulous promises for every believer! God is good! Coach

- One of the most powerful things we can do in our Christian walk- is ask God! In fact, the Bible says: You have not, because you ask not! James 4:2 Our heavenly Father loves when you ask Him for anything! The Lord doesn't get intimidated when you ask Him for really Big things! He says: Ask and you will receive, seek and you will find, and knock and the door shall be opened to you! Matthew 7:7 Since 1988 I have believed and prayed John 14:13-14, more than any verse in the Bible! It says: "And I will do whatever you ask in My name, so that the Father may be glorified in the Son. You may ask me for anything in My name, and I will do it!" What do you need this morning? Ask the Lord and you will see mighty miracles & healing will speedily occur in your life! Isaiah 58:8 Trust and Never Doubt! Coach

- Psalms 91-Has wonderful promises for us, when we enter into His presence!
  1) He will come to our rescue!
  2) He will protect us!
  3) He will Answer & speak to us!
  4) He will be a present help in time of trouble!
  5) He will deliver us from the enemy!
  6) He will assign angels to guard us!
  7) He will honor us to help others!
  8) He will satisfy us- with long life!
  9) He will show us Victory in Salvation!
  I encourage you to pray this chapter over your children and grandchildren every morning! Coach

- The Bible says: "This is the day the lord has made; we will rejoice and be glad in it." Psalms 118:24 Rejoice in the Lord always, I will say it again! Phil. 4:4 The joy of the Lord is my strength! Nehemiah 8:10 Joy is a fruit of the spirit! Galatians 5:22 Smile and laugh all day, because Jesus lives in you! Coach

- All over the world, everyone is looking for peace! You can search and try anything to obtain peace, but only God can provide peace in your heart! I want to share 3 promises that God gives to every believer regarding peace!
  1) Thou will keep Him in perfect peace, whose mind is stayed on thee, because he trust in thee! Isaiah 26:3
  2) And the peace of God, that passes all understanding, shall keep your hearts and minds through Jesus Christ! Phil. 4:6
  3) The Lord Bless you and keep you; the Lord make His face shine upon you, and be gracious to you; the Lord turn His face toward you, and give you peace! Numbers 6:24-26 God knew the exact day you were born, He will never leave you, and He wants you to live stress free! He will calm your spirit and give you peace, TODAY! Coach

- The Bible tell us, if you will do these 2 things, you will get better! 1) Read the Word and practice it daily! Proverbs 4:22
  2) Laugh! Proverbs 17:22
  The Best 2 Medicines you can take in the World! God said it! Coach

- There are many ways to please God, but not one of them will work without faith! You asked: How do I get faith? By hearing the Word of God! Romans 10:17 And Once You Do- Miracles Happen in your life! The Bible says: If you have faith tiny as a mustard seed, you will say to this mountain: move from here to there, and it will move, and nothing will be impossible to you! Matthew 17:20 When you spend time in the Bible- Satan says, it is going to be hard to fool him today, we are going to move on to a lazy Christian! Coach

- This is for someone this morning. You are going to make it! Dark clouds are departing in your life and Heavenly Sunshine is arriving in your life! Just because Jesus Loves you! He revealed it on the cross-You are victorious! Spend time praising Jesus this morning and His presence will restore you! Satan is a liar, don't give him one inch in your life. Cast all your cares on the Lord! Your Best Days Are Ahead! Jesus paid it all! Raise your hands and thank Him! You are going to be just fine! Mark 11:23 Coach

- Truly I want to tell you, whatever you ask for in prayer, believe you have received it, and it will be yours. Mark 11:24 Faith in God always brings the impossible in your life! Faith is the evidence of things unseen. Hebrews 11:1 If you have to see it before you believe it, then God's promises, will not become real in your life. This verse will work for you anytime, anyplace, or anywhere! But there is a condition for this verse to work! Verse 25 says: When you stand praying, if you hold anything against anyone, forgive them, so your Father in Heaven, may forgive your sins! When you forgive- Your prayer life will flourish and you will see mighty miracles! The Bible says so! Coach

- The pain you have been through has given you an entrance into God's Glory! Because if you draw near to Him, He will draw near to you! James 4:8 The Lord will make your most painful experiences, your greatest blessings, if you ask Him to help you! The Lord will take your mess and make it your message, and take your greatest test, and make it your testimony to help others! Jesus is Alive! Coach

- I want to encourage you to laugh more and enjoy your journey! The Bible says: The joy of the Lord is our strength! Nehemiah 8:10 The Bible also says: A joyful heart is an amazing medicine for your entire body and soul! Proverbs 17:22 The Lord promises every believer, He will give us unspeakable joy, if we spend time with Him! John 15:11 Cast all your cares on the Lord, because He cares about you! 1 Peter 5:7 Laugh in the middle of your storm, because you know the Lord is going to do exceedingly, abundantly more for you, than you could ever ask or think! Ephesians 3:20 Call on Jesus- and your life will never be the same! He came to give us life more abundantly! John 10:10 Coach

- David figured out how to beat the Devil, and it is still the only way today! I have hidden your Word in my heart, that I might not sin against you! Psalms 119:11 Read-Study-Memorize the Bible! You will build spiritual muscle to dominate the enemy! Coach

- Life can get so busy. We can let our trials and tribulations weigh us down. We can get in a place where the worries and cares of life overwhelm us. There are faultfinders and gossipers everywhere, don't let them influence you. But I want to tell you tonight, Jesus loves you! He will never leave you! He is eager to make you the best you can be! If you lean on Jesus, He will see you through! The Holy Spirit will give you strength and power to become exactly who God called you to be! I have been through tough times myself, but when you call on Jesus, he will step right in your life just in the nick of time and heal you! 2 Kings 20:5 Coach

- Satan says: "Give Up" Jesus says: "Get Up" God is not through with you yet! He is going to absolutely amaze you, as He gives you more strength than you have ever had! God did not give you a spirit of fear, But of power, love and a sound mind! 2 Timothy 1:7 Coach

- Some of you are going through some stuff tonight. Satan thinks he is going to win. He has said that your past will define you forever. The enemy will try to make you believe your best days are over. Well let's get to the truth, Satan is a liar, and Jesus dominated him on the cross! Jesus will come to your rescue, and deliver you! Psalms 50:15 The Lord will bless you so much, you will become a blessing to others every day! Numbers 6:24-26 The Lord will refresh and restore you! Jeremiah 30:17 The Lord will give you joy unspeakable! John 15:11 This is the greatest day of your life because Jesus never, gives up, on us! He is always there to pick us up and make us whole! Mark 5:34 I just preached myself into the presence of Almighty God! Coach

- In Philippians 4, Paul gives us 5 powerful things that will make us a winner Every day, through the power of the Holy Spirit! You have the ability through Christ, to do these daily!
  1) Rejoice always! Practice this soon as you wake up!
  2) Be anxious for nothing! Don't worry about anything!
  3) Be content in every situation! Don't let anyone steal your joy!
  4) You can do all things! I can't, should never be in your words!
  5) God will supply all your needs! Jesus will meet all your needs!
  The Lord promises you peace that passes all understanding if you are thankful! The only time you will have stress in your life, is when you are not thankful! The Bible says: Stir up the gift of God in you and let your light shine for Him today! Coach

- The Word of God is like its Author- eternal, unchanging, and living! The Word is the mind of Christ, God's actual thought's, and the Will of God! The Word is God speaking. It is a part of God himself. It abides forever. God and His Word are one. John 1:1,14 Jesus is the living Word, and He lives in us, I read the Word; I feed on the Word; and the Word lives in Me! The Word is truth, and it supersedes facts! John 17:17. You may be depressed- But the Word says: be of good cheer! John 16:33 You may have anxiety- But the Word says: Don't worry about anything! Phil. 4:6 You may be sick- But the Word says: I will take sickness away from your midst! Exodus 23:25 You may feel your all alone- But the Word says He will never leave You! Deuteronomy 31:6 You may feel you can't go on- But the Word says: You can do all things through Christ! Phil 4:13 You may feel that God can't forgive you- But the Lord says: I will forgive you instantly & forget your sins! 1 John 1:9, Hebrews 8:12 Refuse to be in the dark anymore and pick up your Bible and God will bring healing to any area of your life, ALWAYS! Proverbs 4:22 Coach

- Jesus tells us the night before He went to the cross: Do not let your heart be troubled. You believe in God; believe also in Me. John 14:1 Then the next verse blows everyone away! My Father's house has many mansions; if that were not so, would I have told you that I am going there to prepare a place before you? He tells us that Heaven is real and He is excited about us going to Heaven! In verse 6, Jesus tells us that He is the only way, truth, and life! There is only one way to go to heaven and it is simply to believe in JESUS! He hung on a cross for all of us! Ask Him into your heart tonight! And your destiny will be secure forever! The Gospel is so powerful! Romans 1:16 Coach

- No one compares to Jesus. He lived here on earth for over 33 years. He never sinned one time, He is the glory of heaven, He is admired by the angels, dreaded by devils, and adored by His children! Spend time with Him in the Word & Prayer, and you will overcome any struggle in your life! Prayer prepares success for your Purpose! 1 Thessalonians 5:16-18 Coach

- No matter how talented, wealthy, educated or cool you think you might be, how you treat people is EVERYTHING! Jesus loves everybody and we should too! Keep loving people and don't let anyone or anything still your joy! Joy comes from the Lord and it will keep you walking in the Spirit even thru the tough times! Nehemiah 8:10 I walked in the flesh for a long time- I not going back- been there done that-Satan is a liar and Jesus will make you whole! What a friend we have in Jesus! Praise makes the enemy insane! Raise your hands and Praise the Lord- You are still breathing! Jesus died on a cross, so we could have an abundant and eternal life! John 10:10 Coach

- Are you trying to comeback from a horrible crisis? I mean, a terrible situation, when everything goes against you in life. Do what Job did in chapter 23 verse 12! You will come out shining on the other side of the storm every time! The Word of God always works, if you work the Word! John 8:31-32 Coach

- Quit beating yourself up over and over, about a past failure or a major mistake. We have all sinned and come short of the glory of God. We have all been in the same boat. Praise God for Jesus! Because of Jesus Blood, every sin we have committed is washed whiter than snow! If you confess your sins, He is faithful and just and will forgive us INSTANTLY, and cleanse us from all unrighteousness! 1 John 1:9. God made him who had no sin to be sin for us, so that in Him we might become the righteousness of God! 2 Corinthians 5:21 Jesus paid the price for us, so we can live a life that honors Him daily. Cast all your cares on the Lord, and get back on your horse, and love and encourage others every day! You have been forgiven and God forgets your sins soon as we repent! Isaiah 43:25 & Hebrews 8:12. We ought to raise our hands and Praise Jesus- We are going to Heaven, not for a trillion years, but forever! If you don't know Jesus, ask Him to come into your life, and He will and He will forgive you and fill you with the Holy Spirit! Jesus came to give us life more abundantly. John 10:10 Coach

- The Bible says if you put the Word first- that means read your Bible daily with the same intensity you do other things you love! It will light up your life and will bring healing to your whole body! I am not making this up, it has worked for me since 1988! Pull out your Bible and dust it off and you can find this PROMISE from God in Proverbs 4:20-22 God's Word will work every time you hide it in your heart! Praise God! Coach

- If we confess our sins, He is faithful and just to forgive us of our sins, and cleanse us from all unrighteousness.1 John1:9
  And He will remember your sins no more. Hebrews 8:12 & Isaiah 43:25
  Get up this morning and know you are forgiven and you are incredibly qualified to be used by the Lord in a miraculous way today! Coach

- There is so much love and healing, where Jesus is looking upon us from Heaven. Did you know Jesus continually intercedes for us (Hebrews 7:25)? The Bible says: "For as the heavens are high above the earth, so great in his mercy (loving kindness) toward those who fear Him." (Psalms 103:11) Surely, beloved, God intends to strengthen us through time in the Word and Prayer! Jesus will turn your weaknesses, into your strengths, and take our unbelief and make it into living faith. The dew of His presence, the power of His love, will be so active upon us that we will be changed by His wonderful Word! I want to encourage you, to go to a place where you will dare to believe that God is waiting to bless you abundantly, beyond all that you can " ask or think." (Ephesians 3:20) Are you ready? What For? You ask. To get before God today with such living faith that you will dare to believe that all things are possible concerning you. (Mark 9:23) Are You Ready? What For? To know today that God's mercy never fails, though we may fail, He is still full of mercy! Are You Ready? Say Yes, and God will surely grant you a very rich blessing, so that you will forget your circumstances, and come into God's bountiful blessings, God wants to bring you into His amazing treasures, He will cover you with His wings of protection! God knew the day you were born, you are so special to the Lord. Your tears of hurt and pain, are going to turn into tears of joy! Your tears will become liquid prayers to our Heavenly Father! Can you say amen! Coach

- Today's Kavanaugh hearing, reminded me of when Jesus died on the cross on Friday and the enemy gloated for 2 days! Satan thought he had all power! But then came Sunday, oh my what a day. Jesus rose from the grave! Dr. Ford was well coached and seems like a nice lady. There is absolutely no evidence to her story, not one person over all these years can stand by her side and say her story is true. Remember this: The Lord is watching over everything, He never sleeps and He knows everything going on! Today the truth came out, and the atmosphere changed! Keep praying, God is going to show up & show out! Satan is a liar, and he hates when people pray for the truth! All smiles here in Hattiesburg! Don't ever let anyone or anything steal your joy! You haven't seen anything yet, God is going to be Glorified! Coach

- If the most wicked man in the whole world will accept Jesus Christ. He will instantly become a new creation, be filled with the Holy Spirit, and go to heaven forever! Jesus came to seek and save the lost! Luke 19:10 Keep praying for others and keep sharing the good news of Jesus Christ! There is enormous POWER in the Blood! Jesus loves everybody and we should too! Coach

- Jesus is the only one that can give you total freedom, healing, and joy unspeakable! There is nothing to difficult for Jesus. The Lord loves to perform His promises for you in the Bible. With faith you can always do the impossible. Once Jesus spoke to a dead man in a casket, and said "Get Up" and the man did and started talking and went home to be a blessing to his mom. No one is like Jesus. Luke 7:11-17 He lives inside of you. Let God use you this weekend. You've got his power. Romans 8:11 & Galatians 2:20. Coach

- One week ago, my Dad was laying on the floor at home, suffering 2 strokes-couldn't walk or talk. But we got everyone praying, and I want to tell each one of you, thank you for praying for my dad! In 48 hours, my dad was walking & talking! Prayer Works- It brings God on the scene-Brings heaven down to earth! The Bible says:" Whatsoever you desire when you pray, believe you have received it, and it will be granted"! Mark 11:24. Jesus means what He says. Don't explain the Bible a way with your doctrine or traditions, just simply take Him at His Word!! Then you will see the same miracles, that you read in the Gospels! In fact, Jesus says, "If you believe in Me, you will do the same miracles that I do and even greater ones, because I go to be with the Father." John 14:12. How is this possible? Jesus lives in you-You have miracle working power in you! Praise the name of Jesus! Dad walks around the hospital the last few days and visits the sick and encourages them! Doctors said this was a true miracle, If Jesus will do this for my Dad, He will do it for you! Acts 10:38. Thanks again 4 your prayers! Love you all! Coach

- This morning as I was praying, the Lord impressed upon me, to tell someone you are close. I mean, closer than close to your miracle! Don't throw in the towel-keep pushing through the obstacles, the heartache and pain. Satan has been working overtime, to keep you defeated. But Satan is a liar. Stay in the race-Jesus is coming to your rescue-don't you dare give up! I really believe today is going to be your breakthrough! The sun is going to shine again, the dark clouds are moving away and God is opening up doors of amazing blessings for you and your family! The Lord is saying, I have spoken to you this morning, that my joy may be in you, and that your joy may be full! John 15:11 Coach

- The Bible says there are 2 words, that can bring amazing miracles in your life! In fact, it is the only spiritual requirement in the Bible, to receive anything from the Lord! Mark 5:36 says:" Do not be afraid any longer, ONLY BELIEVE! It is that simple, but Satan has 2 words to for us too, fear & doubt. So now we are in a spiritual battle who are we going to believe? Jesus or Satan. Well, I turned my back on the Lord for 9 years, and it did not work out well for me. The devil destroyed everything in my life and basically had me on life support. But I called on Jesus, and asked Him to help me, and He put His arms around me, and told me, He still loved me! He, refreshed, revived, and restored me! Within 3 weeks, He told me to pray for the sick, I didn't know He would still heal. I thought you just prayed, if it is your will Lord heal them! That is a lie from hell my friends. Jesus will do anything in the Bible you BELIEVE Him for! Jeremiah 1:12. God's Word is His perfect Will. Find you a verse to cover your case, and your life with Jesus will never be the same! One verse that you act on, has more power than all the power of the enemy! Luke 10:19 You will have joy unspeakable! The Lord will honor His Word 24 hours a day! Your prayer life will become powerful and nothing will be impossible for you all the days of your life! Coach

- Satan will constantly tell you: Give up- You can't make it. The Bible says: Get up- You can do all things through Christ who strengthens you. Phil.4:13 Don't believe the devil's lies only believe God's Word and you will have victory in your life every day! Coach

- The Lord will fight for you, you need only to be still. Exodus 14:14 If you are in a complicated situation with someone, don't get angry and try to get even or one-up someone with your words in your own strength. Did you know, you can let the Lord fight your battles! Be still and put all your worries in God's hand. The quieter you become, and tune out all the noise, you will be able to hear from the Lord in a powerful way! You will be more than a conqueror through Christ! Romans 8:37. Coach

- Jesus is the only one that can give you total freedom, healing, and joy unspeakable! There is nothing too difficult for Jesus. The Lord loves to perform His promises for you in the bible. With faith, you can always do the impossible. Once Jesus spoke to a dead man in a casket, and said "Get Up" and the man did and started talking and went home to be a blessing to his mom. No one is like Jesus. Luke 7:11-17 He lives inside of you. Let God use you this weekend. You've got his power. Romans 8:11 & Galatians 2:20. Coach

- When you accept Jesus as your Savior and Lord, the Holy Spirit comes to live inside of you. You are anointed to do mighty exploits on a level, the world is unfamiliar with, for God's glory! Stop trying to fit in, Jesus wants you to standout for Him. The Lord has given you power through the Holy Spirit, to demolish strongholds and dominate the enemy! Luke 10:19 Coach

- Brothers and Sisters, I have made up my mind to stay in the race for the Lord. I am going to take my place in the winning circle at age 59 and help others go to heaven. But I will finish my race to glorify the Lord. I have made up my mind to let God's love flow through me to encourage anyone that is struggling! I have made up my mind to quit leaving Jesus out of my everyday affairs. We know that Jesus is coming back soon- We don't have any time to play games anymore. It is time to let our light shine for Christ! I have made up my mind to pray for hurting people at Walmart or at my church! When we are determined and committed to serve Jesus- You will all be filled with the Holy Spirit! Fear-Anger-Gossip- Will be far from you. His AMAZING Grace will make you love your enemies! Laughter and Joy from the Lord will fill you days, and miracles will be a regular occurrence in your walk with the Lord! Satan lies to us every day, he says, don't get close to Jesus, you will miss so much in life. For your information Satan is going to get thrown in the lake of fire! Jesus says: Come unto me who are weary and heavy laden and I will give you rest! One day, we will all see Jesus face to face and He will judge us, and if you have believed in Jesus, He will say "Come on in, you believed in my Son! Tell everyone about Jesus! Coach

- It only takes 1 verse! One verse is all it takes to get saved, healed, or get your breakthrough! You see every verse has been breathed by the Holy Spirit! 1) If you believe John 3:16- You go to heaven! 2) If you believe Psalms 103:3- You get Healed! 3) If you believe Matthew 11:28- You get total rest! 4) If you believe Isaiah 26:3- You get perfect peace! 5) If you believe John 8:32- You get set free! Hebrews 4:12 says the Word is alive and is sharper than a two-edge sword! The Word will work 24 hours a day! The Lord will honor His Word always! Open your Bible and God will speak to you! Coach

- Romans 12:12 says: Rejoice in hope, be patient in affliction, be persistent in prayer. The Great Physician's 3 prescriptions for tough times!
    1. Rejoice in Hope-Despite current conditions. The son is shining for me as brightly as ever with Healing in His rays! Isaiah 58:8
    2. Be patient in Affliction- It is the ability to wait calmly, as the Lord works everything for my good! Romans 8:28 & Isaiah 40: 28-31
    3. Be persistent in Prayer- An open Bible and a bowed head, create a powerful atmosphere in which God's will is brought to beat upon the distresses of life! 1 Thess. 5:17 1 John 5:14-15

Romans 12:12- Is a shot in the arm for whatever ails you!

Psalms 34:19- God will deliver you out of any affliction- always! Coach

- The Bible says that every knee shall bow and every tongue will confess that Jesus is Lord. Everyone who lived on earth will give an account of themselves to God. Romans 14:11-12. If you believe that Jesus is the Son of God and you simply ask Him into your heart- you go to heaven forever! If someone never believed in Jesus on Earth, you go to hell. Jesus is the only way to heaven! John 14:6. I don't want the Lord to tell anyone on judgement day-depart from me I never knew you. Matthew 7:23. So friends, we've got some work to do! Jesus uses people like you and me to tell others about Jesus! God uses people that are flawed and a work in progress to share the Gospel! We have been forgiven and we have the Holy spirit to help us be bold for the Lord. Nothing in life really matters, except having assurance you have eternal life! It is time for you and me to fight for the Lord like we are the third monkey trying to get on Noah's Ark!!! Get pumped up! Coach

- If you feel like you have been a failure in your Christian walk and your life is in a dark place. I have some good news. You are still the apple of God's eye. If you were the only person on earth, Jesus would have still died for you! God will never count you out-He will never leave you or forsake you. He will redeem your life, no matter how big of a mess you have made. You are one-of-a-kind and God has a perfect plan for your life. Humpty Dumpty went to the wrong king, come to Jesus and He will put you back together again! I had to do it. He will give all your dreams back to you and fill you with His precious Holy Spirit. He made the whole world in six days and rested on the seventh. There is nothing too difficult for God! He will make a way when there is no way! Call on Him today. The Lord will hear from heaven and forgive you and heal you! Have a fantastic weekend!
Coach

- I want to be honest, as I can this morning. I have failed the Lord, and turned my back on Him so many times. But as I get older and a little wiser, spending time with the Lord in Prayer and in the Word is the greatest joy in my life! Through the years, the Lord has taught me how to have a great day-even when the storms are all around. I am going to give you four truths this morning to have an abundant life!
1) Be kind and compassionate to others! Ephesians 4:32
2) Don't whine or complain! Philippians 2:14
3) Forgive and Forget! Colossians 3:13
4) Don't let anyone or anything steal your joy! Nehemiah 8:10 & Philippians 4:4
Today is the greatest day of your life because Jesus lives in you!
Let's Win Today! Coach

- Wishing for things in your life to come to pass is a good thing. Wishing can create dreams in your life. Faith on the other hand, pleases God and activates God's power into your life! Faith in God creates the impossible to become reality in your life! Matthew 17:20 In Mark 5:25-34 talks about a lady who suffered for 12 years with an incurable disease. She went to every doctor, spent all her money, and instead of getting better she got worse. But she heard that Jesus was coming to her town, and she said, "When I touch His clothes, I will be healed! Soon as she touched Jesus garment, power flowed into her! Why did she get healed? Many people touched Him, Jesus was walking in a huge crowd. All the others were wishing, this sweet lady had faith! Wishing and True Faith are miles apart, if you need a touch from the Lord. Your faith will make you whole. He rewards those who diligently seek Him! Hebrews 11:6 Coach

- Let us not get weary in doing good, for at the proper time you will reap a harvest, if you do not give up. Galatians 6:9 Persistence is a firm continuance in a course of action in spite of difficulty or opposition. Don't go back to being a lukewarm Christian. Your greatest breakthrough in your life is in sight! Your best days are ahead! It is simply how bad you want it, be Relentless like Paul in the Bible. Don't let the enemy cheat you out of the things the Lord has in store for you. Don't let Satan steal your joy. Rise up and say, as for me and my house, we will serve the Lord! Joshua 24:15 Blessing will chase you down! Coach

- The Bible tell us, if you will do these 2 things, you will get better! 1) Read the Word and practice it daily! Proverbs 4:22
  2) Laugh! Proverbs 17:22
  The Best 2 Medicines you can take in the World! God said it! Coach

- We have all gone through some tough situations, hard trials, and struggles in our lives. Some of you are trying to get over a bitter and painful relationship, some of you have lost a loved one, and your heart is broken, and others have gone through a season where the devil has ripped your life apart. The Bible says, God is a very present help in time of trouble. Psalms 46:1. The Lord will refresh, renew, revive, and restore you! He has done it for me over and over. If you are this- God woke you up this morning, you are breathing, alive, and totally loved by god who knew the exact day you came out of your mother's womb! Cast all your cares on the Lord because He cares for you! 1 Peter 5:7. He says in Isaiah 40:31- those who trust in the Lord will find new STRENGTH, they will soar on wings like an eagle again! God has given you the power to walk out of this nightmare right now! God is light and in Him is NO darkness! 1 John 1:5. God is telling you everything is going to be alright- Trust Him. Put a smile on your face, and go tell others what the Lord has done for You! Coach

- Heaven is real, it is not a myth or a fairy tale. If you accept the free gift of eternal life through Jesus Christ, you will live there forever! This morning, I want to share a few verses about heaven.
    1. For the Lord himself will come down from heaven, with a loud command, with the voice of an archangel and with the trumpet call of God, and the dead in Christ will rise first. After that, we who are still alive and are left will be caught up together with them in the clouds to meet the Lord in the air. And we will be with the Lord forever. 1 Thessalonians 4:16-17

    2. My Father's house has many mansions, if that were not so, would I have told you that I am going to prepare a place for you. John 14:2

    3. Set your mind on things above, not earthly things. Colossians 3:2

4. But our citizenship is in heaven, and we eagerly wait our savior from there, the Lord Jesus Christ. Philippians 3:20

5. The Lord will rescue me from every evil attack and will bring me safely to His heavenly kingdom. To Him be the glory for ever and ever! Amen. 2 Timothy 4:18

6. I encourage you to pray for loved ones, co-workers and friends that don't know the Lord. May the Holy Spirit give you boldness to share the Greatest Love Story of all time! Jesus came to seek and save the lost! Luke 19:10

7. The Bible says: I tell you that in the same way, there will be more rejoicing in heaven over one sinner who repents than over ninety-nine righteous persons who do not need to repent! Luke 15:7

Let God use you today to bring someone else to heaven! Coach

- If you want to be more than a conqueror through Christ-What you do on a daily basis is the key! We have a decision to make each morning. Here are a few ways you can get stronger and more vibrant in your Christian walk. Read God's Word Daily. No Word-No Breakfast. Matthew 4:4 Keep hearing the Word as it creates faith to have victory. Romans 10:17 Speak the Word. Death and life are in the power of the tongue. Proverbs 18:21 Your words are either faith filled or fear filled. Speak healing over your children! Control your thought life. We are either meditating on Satan's lies of God's promises. Joshua 1:8 and Proverbs 4:20-22 Worship and Praise the Lord Daily! We are called to praise the Lord at all times. Psalms 34:1. Victory always comes after praise! Miracles happen after Praise! Get rid of Baggage. God forgives you instantly when you confess your sins! 1 John 1:9 and Romans 8:1. Don't let past failures and mistakes weigh you down. God remembers your sins no more! Hebrews 8:12 and Isaiah 43:25 Have a fantastic day. Smile and Laugh all day. Encourage someone today! Jesus set us Free! Coach

- We are in a spiritual battle, and we get to choose each day to be led by the spirit or walk in the flesh. Everyone has been bruised, nicked up, and has some battle scars because we decided not to put the Lord first in our lives. Some of you feel like you are losing the battle, and others are under an assault of the enemy today. I want to let you know we are a work in progress, none of us are perfect. But I want to encourage you to get back on your horse and fight the good fight of faith! I sense an outpouring of God's Spirit on us like we have never known. There is a king in you, visions to decree, demons to dominate, and Goliaths to defeat! The Lord is making his face to shine upon you. Numbers 6:24-26. We will not go back to our old sin nature- been there done that. It is time for you and me to resist the devil, and let the Lord fill us with the Holy Spirit We are going to show God's love everywhere we go, to help and encourage hurting people. Let's put on the whole armor of God and dominate the enemy Ephesians 6:10-17. With Jesus we have all we need to win this battle. Let's roll! Jesus is coming back soon. Coach

- It is only through Jesus Christ that a person can be saved. Anyone who rejects Jesus Christ will experience eternal punishment in hell. The Bible describes hell as: A place of flames. Luke 16:24 A place of physical torment with burning fire. Revelations 21:8 A place of darkness. Matthew 8:12 22:13 25:50 2 Peter 2:17 Jude 13 A fiery furnace Matthew 13:42-43 A place banished from God's presence. Matthew 24:51 22:13 7:23 As Christians, we need to share Jesus with others? We have family members, friends, and co-workers that don't know the Lord! It is time for us to tell everyone about Jesus! Let me tell you exactly how you can escape hell. The Bible says, " For God so loved the world that He gave his only begotten Son, that whosoever will believe in Him, shall not perish, but he shall have eternal life! John 3:16 Call on Jesus tonight and you will be saved, it is in the Bible! Acts 2:21 Don't go to bed until you make sure you are going to heaven! Share this with every friend you have! Coach

- There is more power in one verse that you believe in and act on, than all the power of the enemy! Luke 10:19

If you believe John 3:16 You will have eternal life!

If you believe Matthew 11:28 You will have total rest!

If you believe John 8:32- You will be totally free!

If you believe Jeremiah 33:3- You will see mighty miracles!

If you believe James 1:5 -You will have God's wisdom!

If you believe Luke 1:37- Nothing will be impossible to you!

If you believe John 14:13- You will have a powerful prayer life!

If you believe John 15:11- You will have unspeakable joy!

If you believe Joshua 1:8- You will have great success!

If you believe Phil. 4:13- You can accomplish anything!

For no matter, how many promises of God has made, they are yes in Christ! 2 Corinthians 1:20

Take your two hands and open up your Bible, and God will speak to you! Coach

- I want to assure you, that you are not wasting your time when you pray. James 5:16 says the prayer of a Christian is powerful and effective! I make my request known before you in the morning and wait in expectation! Psalms 5:3 In August of 1976, my grandmother prayed over me the day before she died. And you know what- Over 42 years later that prayer is still is working in my life! Keep praying over your kids and grandkids!! Coach

- I know for some of you 2018 has been the toughest year of your life. I pray that God will give you strength like you have never known before! He will do it for you! Psalms 138:3 One thing I do know! If we will spend time in the Bible, and with Jesus! The Holy Spirit will help you flip the page, and bring forth an incredible new chapter in your life in 2019! Your best days are ahead! Jeremiah 29:11 Coach

- Life is so short. I will turn 60 next year. It seems like yesterday, I was playing Little League Baseball. I have made more mistakes and turned my back on Jesus so many times. But I have made my mind up- I not going back! Been There- Done That! Jesus brought me out of Satan's trap! I will never go back! Jesus is my best friend! I got to go- I could preach all night! John 10:10 Coach

- No matter what you are facing-God will always bring you out! Anxiety & Depression is going to leave you like dew in the morning! Your smile and laughter are coming back stronger than ever! God is giving you a new song to sing everywhere you go! People are going to be amazed at what Jesus did for you! Psalms 40:1-3 Coach

- God's Word is God's perfect will. When you open up the Bible and read it, you are learning God's will in any situation. The Bible says: The unfolding of your words give light, it gives understanding to the simple. Psalms 119:130 Until we have a verse to cover our case, we will always be in the dark. The Bible will enlighten you as you find the promise you need for every situation. Every answer to every problem is in the Bible! In fact, the Bibles says the only wat to overcome sin in your life is storing the Word and hiding it in your heart! Psalms 119:11 When you read and study the Bible, you get God's thoughts for anything you need. The greatest place a Christian can be in, is standing on the promises of God! The Lord He says: He is watching over His Word to perform it in your life! Jeremiah 1:12 The Word is alive, it will work 24 hours a day. Keep staying in the Word, and you will hear from Heaven and know His will. Coach

- I am going to give you 5 verses that I have acted on, and have seen the Lord do mighty miracles over the past 30 years!
  1) And I will do whatever you ask in my name, so that the Father may be glorified in the Son, you may ask me anything in My name, and I will do it. John 14:13-14
  2) Call to Me, and I will answer you, and I will tell you great and mighty things that you have not Known. Jeremiah 33:3
  3) If you abide in Me, and My words abide in you, ask whatever you wish and it will be done for you. John 15:7
  4) Until now you have not asked for anything in My name, ask and you will receive and your joy will be complete. John 15:11
  5) Again, truly I tell you if two of you on earth about anything they ask for, it will be done for them by My Father in Heaven. Matthew 18:19

Asking god is so powerful, He loves when you ask Him to help you! He is eager to perform any of His promises in the Bible when you ask Him. I wouldn't even be married if I hadn't asked my wife! The Lord wants you to live in victory, these promises will help you each day. Coach

- Smile Today and Uplift Someone's Spirit
  1. A cheerful heart brings joy to the soul, good news makes for good health. Proverbs 15:30
  2. A joyful heart is good medicine, but depression drain's one strength, Proverbs 17:22
  3. A glad heart makes a happy face, a broken heart crushes the spirit. Proverbs 15:13
  4. Laughter will create joy and you will see that the Lord has done great things for us. Psalms 126:2-3
  5. Count it all joy, my brothers, when you face various trials, for you know that the testing of your faith produces patience, that you may be complete, lacking in nothing. James 1:2-4
  6. Pray this over you every morning-Lord, let your face shine upon me, and teach me Your Word! Psalms 119:35
  7. When you walk with the Lord, you can laugh in the middle of the storm, because you know He will deliver You to safety every time! Psalms 34:19 Smile all day! Encourage Yourself! Coach

- Jesus was never in a hurry. He was never afraid. He never showed weakness. He was always ready. He never hesitated. He was always sure. He knew who He was. He knew the Father. He knew about Heaven. He knew where He was going. He had no lack. He had no defeat. He was almighty-yet just a man! And he lives in you! Galatians 2:20 When I put the Lord 1st in my life, I love all my enemies and laugh all day! Phil. 4:11 Coach

- The Word of God can change any crisis you are going through. Go to the Bible, and find chapter and verse, and you will have a Promise from God! We all go through tough times. The Bible says to consider it all joy when this happens! James 1:2 Paul said: I have learned to be content in every single situation- Good or Bad! Phil. 4:11 How? Because the Bible says: Many are the afflictions of every Christian-But He delivers us out of them ALL! Psalms 34:19 Smile, help is on the way! Coach

- Jesus laid down His life for us, He loved us so much that He was mocked, beaten, and hung on a cross. He shed His blood so that every single person who believes in Him, will have eternal life! The Lord gives us free will, that means we have to believe Jesus is the Son of God and confess that you want Him to be Lord and Savior of your life. Romans 10:8-10 and John 3:16 When you ask Jesus into your heart, you will live in Heaven forever! If you have a loved one, co-worker, or a friend who is not saved, God wants to use you to share God's love! Get on your knees and ask the Lord for boldness to share the gospel to others! One day every knee shall bow, and every tongue will confess Jesus is Lord! Everyone on this earth will one day see Jesus face to face! Make sure your name is written in the Book of Life today! Luke 10:20 Coach

- It was Jesus scars that convinced "Doubting Thomas", and your scars may be the message that convinces someone that they too can overcome! John 20:25 You brought your wounds to Jesus, now He is using your scars to minister to others! Amazing Grace! God will take your mess and make it your message! He will take your test and make it your testimony! He will take your pain and make you a great problem solver! Jesus will make a Way when there is No Way! You made it through the rain, Sunshine is on the way! Coach

- The Bible says: Death and Life are in the power of the tongue! Proverbs 18:21 Your words are so important to have a successful Christian walk! God uses words to create! He used His words to frame the world. Hebrews 11:3 Words are containers, they carry life and healing or hurt and pain. Your words can encourage someone or discourage someone. When you say kind words, you can change the atmosphere for the good! When you speak the promises of God, you will encourage yourself! Say this out loud, Today is the greatest day of my life, because Jesus lives in me! Galatians 2:20 Coach

- Jesus says: Come to me, all who are weary and heavy laden, and I will give you rest! Matthew 11:28 The Bible also says: Cast all your cares on Me, because I care about you. 1 Peter 5:7 Jesus wants you to be mentally and emotionally well. The Lord will pick up all your broken pieces an put you back together again! He will help you become strong, vibrant, and totally whole! 1 Thessalonians 5:23 When you get in the Lord's presence, anxiety and depression will melt away like snow! Phil. 4:6 He will make you lie down in green pastures and lead you by still waters! Psalms 23:2-3 Coach

- There is only one thing God cannot do- Remember your sins, when you ask Him to forgive you! Hebrews 8:12 & Isaiah 43:25 If there was a scoreboard in Heaven keeping up with your sins, and God pulled up your name, your sins would be zero, if you have invited Jesus in your heart! Because Jesus shed His blood on the cross, so that all your sins could be washed away whiter than snow! Romans 8:1 Jesus is the only way to go to Heaven! John 14:6 Rejoice and Praise Jesus! Coach

- We Serve a Big God! God made the world in 6 days and rested on the 7th. If you were in a rocket traveling 30,000 MPH it would take you-around 50 minutes to go around the earth-8 hours to get to the Moon- over 4 months to get to the Sun- 6.5 months to get to Mars-9.5 years to get to Pluto- to get to the nearest star (Proxima Centauri) it would take over 90,000 years! The Lord is big enough to take care of all your problems, heartache, and pain! Call on Him, He sent His only son Jesus for you! Coach

- God did mighty miracles all through the Bible. Here are some of them, and I want you to know that He wants to do them through you. John 14:12

1) He made a donkey speak with human words. Numbers 22:28

2) He rained down bread & quail for the Israelites for 40 years. Exodus 10

3) He parted the Red Sea through Moses. Exodus 14:21

4) He made the Sun & Moon stand still for almost a day for Joshua. Joshua 10: 12-13

5) He went into a fiery furnace and protected 3 men who trusted Him. Daniel 3:19-27

I want to share a verse that will blow your mind! Jesus did many other things as well, if every one of them were written down, I suppose that even the whole world would not have room for the Books that would be written. John 21:25 Seek the Lord daily and spend time in the Word and you will see mighty miracles! Coach

- God will never ask you to have faith for anything that he hasn't already promised in the Bible. You see, if you can do it on your own, it doesn't require faith. God's promises will never fail, if you act like they are real. The Bible says, put the Word first in your life, and it will bring healing to your whole body! Proverbs 4:22 In the beginning was the Word, the Word was with God, the Word was God. John 1:1 They are inseparable. If you want to get closer to God, read the Bible. The Word became flesh which is Jesus. John 1:14 Jesus is the physical expression of the will of God. That is why it is paramount to stay in the Word. The Word is our spiritual food to produce spiritual muscles. God is watching over His Word to perform it in your life. Jeremiah 1:12 Find a verse and hold on to it with a bulldog faith. And you will see the Lord move on your behalf. Keep standing on the Promises of God and you will be a winner every time! Coach

- You may feel like your world has been torn apart. You may have been through hell and high water. You may have experienced so much pain and heartache, you can't tell anyone your story. The enemy has been telling you, you can't make it, throw in the towel, you are finished, it is all over. Let's get something straight, Satan is a liar. Jesus says, I want to give you everything you need to win this race! 1 Corinthians 9:24 God says, A bruised reed I will not break, and a smoldering wick I will not snuff out. Isaiah 42:3 God says, No weapon formed against you will prosper. Isaiah 54:17 The Bible also says, I have given you everything you need to live a life that pleases Me, it was all given to you by My own Power. 2 Peter 1:3 Coach

- God says, New things are going to take place in your life, and I will announce them to you, before they happen. Isaiah 42:9 God is on your side, you are not alone! Say bye-bye to your heartache and pain. Lift your hands and praise your Heavenly Father! Your painful setback, has produced your Greatest Comeback! Laugh and smile in the devil's face. You are going to make it! Coach

- If the most wicked man in the whole world will accept Jesus Christ. He will instantly become a new creation, be filled with the Holy Spirit, and go to heaven forever! Jesus came to seek and save the lost! Luke 19:10 Keep praying for others and keep sharing the good news of Jesus Christ! There is enormous POWER in the Blood! Jesus loves everybody and we should too! Coach

- How do we have joy when we are going through trials and tribulations? James 1:2 Because God promises to every believer that many are the afflictions of the righteous: but the Lord delivers them out of them all! Psalms 34:19 God is our deliverer, and He will always give us a perfect pathway to total VICTORY! Praise the Lord right now-Your Breakthrough is on the way! Coach

- The greatest prayer you can pray; is like David. Let me hear joy and gladness... Create in me a clean heart, 0 God, and renew a right spirit in me! Do not cast me from your presence or take your Holy Spirit away from me! Restore to me the joy of my salvation and grant me a willing spirit, to sustain me! Psalms 51:8-12 Then You will never say anything negative again! Gossip, whining, and complaining will never enter your mouth! And Your Best Days will surely Be Ahead! You will be a light in the middle of darkness! 1 John 1:5 Coach

- I wanted Billy Graham to live to be a hundred years old! But now I know why he lived to be 99." What do you think? If a man owns a hundred sheep, and one of them wanders away, will he not leave the Ninety-Nine on the hills and go look for the one that wandered off?" Matthew 18:12 Billy Graham always, loved the 99, but was used by the Lord to minister to the ONE that was lost! I really believe the greatest revival is coming soon! Praise His Name! Coach

- There are 2 verses that come to my mind tonight about Jesus. Jesus went through Galilee, teaching in their synagogues, preaching the gospel of the kingdom and healing every disease and sickness among the people. Matthew 4:23 How God anointed Jesus of Nazareth with the Holy Spirit and power, and how He went around doing good and healing all who were under the power of the devil, because God was with Him! Acts 10:38 The Bible says Jesus is the same yesterday, today, and FOREVER! Hebrews 13:8 What are you waiting on? Jesus will save you and heal you tonight! He is always ready to do exceedingly, abundantly more than we can ever ask or think, through His power that works within us! Ephesians 3:20 Coach

- God told me to write this and pray this over my friends today! This is a new day for you! A New Beginning! A time to turn the page and start a new chapter in your life. A chapter which says: " Behold, I am about to do something new; Now it will spring forth! Do you not see it? I will make a way in the wilderness and streams in the desert for you." Isaiah 43:19 Today the Lord is saying to you, it is a time for refreshing, your dry season is over! I will make your cup to overflow with blessings, and fill your days with love and laughter! My healing is springing forth in your life, so you can be a blessing to others! Isaiah 58:8 You will live by faith and not by sight for the rest of your life! 2 Corinthians 5:7 And Nothing will be impossible for you and your family all the days of your life! Luke 1:37 Coach

- The Gospel is Good News, thank the Lord for saving us! God wants you to enjoy your walk with the Lord! Here are some beautiful passages to memorize! 1) Whoever believes in Jesus Christ shall not perish, but have eternal life! John 3:16 2) Anyone who believes on the Son has everlasting life! John 3:36 3) Jesus said, I have come that you might have life more abundantly! John 10;10 4) When God the Father, with glorious power, brought Jesus Christ back to life again, you were given His wonderful new life to enjoy, now you share His new life! Romans 6:4-5 5) So look upon your old sin nature as dead, and instead be alive to God through Jesus Christ! Romans 6:11 6) Jesus Christ's divine power has given unto us all things that pertain unto life! 2 Peter 1:3 7) God remembers our sins no more! Hebrews 8:12 Laugh and smile all day! Jesus paid it all! Coach

- Do not judged, and you will not be judged. Do not condemn and you will not be condemned. Forgive and you will be forgiven. Luke 6:37 This verse has so much wisdom for you and me. Keep encouraging others and lifting them up! I have made so many mistakes in my life, how could I have the audacity to judge someone! Always See the best in others and forgive them and pray for them and you will find healing! James 5:16 says so. Heaven would be empty if not for the amazing grace of forgiveness that Jesus paid for on the cross! He loves us so much! I can praise Him all day long! Coach

- How do we make the Word of God alive and real in our life? Speak the Word, and then you own it, and it will accomplish mighty things in your life! 55:11 The Bible says, when we read the Word, we will then know the truth, and the truth will make you free! John 8:31-32 Remember one verse that you put in your heart is more powerful than all the power of the enemy! The Word is the greatest medicine you can take for your well-being Proverbs 4:20-22 Coach

- Jesus loves you and he showed it on the cross! He wants to be your best friend! One of the greatest places we can be in, is when we are desperate and have no other options, but to call on Jesus! Jeremiah 33:3 says: Call upon Me, and I will answer you, and I will show you great and mighty things, that you don't know. I want to tell you Jesus is real, and He will make a way for you. when there is no way! Jesus will clean up any mess you have made! He will forgive you, and put your feet back on solid ground! He will help you press through heartache and pain, to get to your perfect destiny! He will provide anything you need to be a blessing to others! Jesus will heal you in any area of your life! Jesus will give you perfect peace and unspeakable joy! You can try anything in this world, I did, but Jesus is the only answer! Jesus will make you whole and you will never be discouraged again! He is a very present help in time of trouble! Psalms 46:1. Trust and Never doubt, Jesus will always bring you through. Coach

- If God says: I am the Lord who heals you, and you dare to believe the power of these wonderful words, you will act on them! Exodus 15:26 The creative power of God's Word will create the very thing in your mind or body that you need in order to be well and strong! God watches over His Word to perform it, night and day! Jeremiah 1:12 Your weakness will be transformed into strength! Psalms 27:1 Faith without works is dead. James 2:26 All we have to do is take Jesus at His Word and Miracles happen! Quit leaning on your own understanding, and just trust the Lord! The Lord will put you back together again! Humpty Dumpty went to the wrong king! Call on Jesus! Coach

- Here are a number of blessings that God provides for all His children. But we must open up the Bible and find them, and align ourselves with His precious promises. 1) We never have to worry again. Phil. 4:6 & 1 Peter 5:7 2) We are never alone. Hebrews 13:5 3) We will live forever and ever. John 3:16 & John 10:28-30 4) God will supply every need we have. Phil 4:19 5) We can do all things through Christ. Phil. 4:13 6) By His Stripes we are healed. Isaiah 53:4-5 7) We can have unspeakable Joy. John 15:11 & 1 Peter 1:8 8) We can have peace that passes all understanding. Phil. 4:7 9) We can have every desire of our heart. Psalms 34:7 10) God has angels in charge concerning us. Psalms 91:11 11) He will give us perfect rest. Matthew 11:28-30 12) We can resist the devil, and he has to flee. James 4:7 13) When we act on the Word, we become successful Joshua 1:8 14) God has made us for the impossible. Matthew 17:20 15) With long life He will satisfy us. Psalms 91:16 God never breaks one word of His Promises! 1 Kings 8:56 Trust Him today with your whole heart, and the Lord will make all your paths straight! Proverbs 3:5-6 Coach

- Genuine faith in God and His Word, is stepping out upon what He has said regardless of what one sees, feels, or senses in the natural. Faith ignores every natural symptom or evidence which is contrary to what God's Word states! Hebrews 11:6 Faith is simply believing that God will do exactly what He says in His Word, He would do! The Bible says, if you have faith as tiny as a mustard seed, you can tell a mountain to move and it will move, and nothing shall be impossible all the days of your life. Matthew 17:20 Remember faith only comes one way, by hearing the Word of God. Romans 10:17 Faith always wins, it always puts the Word over your situations. Mark 5:34 God always acts on your behalf when you trust Him! Proverbs 3:5-6 Coach

- Persistence is a firm continuance in a course of action in spite of difficulty or opposition. If we really want a successful walk with Jesus and see him do mighty works through us, we must be persistent. It is really how bad you want it. Doubt will put you on an emotional roller coaster. The Bible says that we will be like a wave blown and tossed by the wind. James 1:5-8 All we have to do is have a child like faith. Trust the Lord and do not retreat. Blind Bartimaeus had to do it. He shouted "Jesus son of David have mercy on me!" Many rebuked him and told him to shut up. Bartimaeus did not care. He was persistent and he shouted louder. Sometimes we have to keep going, keep plowing ahead, keep fighting, push through public opinion and pain. Jesus asked him, "What do you want from me?" He said, "I want to see!" Jesus said, "Go, your faith has healed you." Don't throw in the towel, Keep the faith and you will see your miracle! Coach

- The Bible says to resist the devil and he will flee from you! James 4:7 That means to tell him NO when he tempts us! The Bible also says, every good and perfect gift comes from the Lord from Heaven! James 1:17 So anything that is not in heaven you need to resist! When doubt comes- resist it! When fear comes- resist it! When sickness comes- resist it! Satan comes to kill, steal, and destroy. Jesus comes to give you an abundant life! John 10:10 It is all up to you who you are going to believe, the devil and his lies, or God's promises. The Lord will turn your situation around tonight. Matthew 8:17 & Proverbs 4:20-22 Coach

- The Bible says we can't please God without faith. Hebrews 11:6 So this morn I will share about faith. Faith is the substance of things hoped for, the evidence of things not seen. Hebrews 11:1 Faith comes only one way- "Faith comes by hearing, hearing by the Word of God" Romans 10:17 When you open up your Bible and read the Word, faith will enter your heart and you will begin to have a winning attitude! The Bible says: " If you have faith tiny as a mustard seed, you can say to this mountain, move from here to there, and it will move, and nothing will be impossible to you." Matthew 17:20 Having faith in God changes everything in your life! Instead of being a victim, you become a victor! Trust the Lord this morning, keep fighting, you are going to see God intervene in your situation! Your Best Days are Ahead! God loves you so much, He is coming to your rescue! Everything is working out for your good! Romans 8:28. Give thanks to the Lord, He woke you up this morning and He has a perfect plan for you! Jeremiah 29:11 Jesus will heal you in any area of your life, ask Him right now! Mark 9:23 Faith sees the answer before it shows up in your life! Praise the Lord! Coach

- God gives every Christian 9 attributes through the Holy Spirit. These are the fruit of the Spirit, " Love, Joy, Peace, Long Suffering, Kindness, Goodness, Faithfulness, Gentleness, and Self-Control." Galatians 5:22 God wants to work each one of these 9 fruits into our personality- to change us and to change others around us! He wants us to be light in a crazy and dying world, where we literally radiate with the presence of God. The Holy Spirit is a gentleman, He gives us free will and He will never force His way on us. That is why we must allow the Holy Spirit to have His way in us! Being led by the Holy Spirit, is something we continue to grow in each day. As we mature as a Christian, we become more and more sensitive to the Lord's leadership! We are able to be still, and eliminate the chaos in our life, and hear the Lord's still small voice! The Holy Spirit will lead you to total victory in your life!

The Bible says: It is not by power or by might but by my Spirit says the Lord! Zechariah 4:6. All of us should take an inventory and make sure the fruit of the Spirit is transparent in our lives. Ask the Lord to fill you with His Spirit today, put on the armor of God and become a warrior for the Lord! He will use you in a mighty way! God is going to show the whole world His Power -because He is light and in Him there is no darkness! 1 John 1:5 Coach

- Refrain from gossip and stay away from those who practice it. If you can't say something publicly, don't say it at all. Gossipers and faultfinders are on every street corner. You keep encouraging and uplifting others and God's blessings will chase you down! Ephesians 4:29-32 Coach

- Encourage Yourself this morning by simply believing some of God's precious promises: 1) All My sins are forgiven. 1 John 1:9 2) God forgets every sin I have ever committed. Hebrews 8:12 3) I can do all things through Christ. Phil. 4:13 4) My God shall supply all my needs. Phil. 4:19 5) God will give me every desire of my heart. Psalms 34:7 6) The Lord will deliver me out of every affliction. Psalms 34:19 7) He pours His love into my heart. Romans 5:5 8) Greater is He that is in me, than He that is in the world. 1 John 4:4 9) I can ask anything in Jesus name, and He will do it. John 14:13-14 10) He will heal all my diseases. Psalms 103:3 11) He will give me strength, to soar like an eagle. Isaiah 40:31 12) God sent his Son, so we could have eternal life! John 3:16 13) He will take sickness away from your midst. Exodus 23:25 14) Do not be afraid any longer, ONLY BELIEVE. Mark 5:36 15) All things are possible to the believer. Luke 1:37 16) Nothing is impossible with Christ. Matthew 17:20 17) Resist the devil, and he has to flee. James 4:7

- 18) You are more than a conqueror thru Christ. Romans 8:37 19) God will never leave you or forsake you. Hebrews 13:5 20) God is a very present help in time of trouble. Psalms 46:1 There are thousands of promises in the Bible, the Holy Spirit will perform any promise that you believe and act on in your life! When the storms of life come you will have a tremendous advantage if you memorize scripture! Because God's will is His Word! You will have God's thoughts already in your heart! Coach

- Jesus wants to brighten up your life like the rising sun. The Bible says: God has poured out His love into our hearts through the Holy Spirit. Romans 5:5. Love is not love until you show it- a bell is not a bell until you ring it. We must love others, because we have God's love in us. The secret to walking in the spirit, is loving our enemies. We can never do this by walking in the flesh. Satan uses 2 weapons to keep us in bondage, holding grudges and not forgiving others. The Bible says: " But I tell you, love your enemies and pray for those who persecute you, that you may be children of your Father in heaven." Matthew 5:43-48. Because of God's amazing grace that forgave us, we can forgive others also. When you do this, you will encourage people everywhere you go! Worries, cares, and gossip will be so far from you. Heavenly sunshine will be on you night and day! Your prayer life will become so powerful, because your faith will be working through God's love. Galatians 5:6. You will see the best in everyone you come in contact with. Jealousy, envy, and pride will melt away like snow in your life. Jesus compassion will fill your life so strong, that you will feel God's love to help everyone. You will be able to love-the unlovable! Joy will radiate into your life and nothing will be impossible for you all the days of your life! Nehemiah 8:10 & Matthew 17:20 Coach

- 3 John 2 gives the will of God for you. " Beloved, I wish above all things that you may prosper, and be in health, as your soul prospers." God wants you to be whole spiritually, emotionally, and physically! In Psalms 1:3 The Bible says: " but whoever delights in the Word of God, and who meditates on it day and night. That person will be like a tree planted by streams of water, which yields its fruit in season, and whose leaf does not wither- whatever they do prospers." Joshua 1:8 says: " Keep the Word of God always on your lips; meditate on it day and night, so that you may be careful to do everything written in it. Then you will be prosperous and successful!" Put the Word of God into practice, so when the storms of life come, you will be unshakable, unbreakable, immovable! You will be well built for any assignment the Lord gives you! Luke 6:47-48. God's blessings don't fall on us automatically, we have apart to play too! Make up your mind to be a doer of the Word, and God's blessings will chase you down! God's blessings will come in like a flood! James 1:12,25. Coach

- Over the last 30 years, God has asked me to pray for the sick. When the Lord started to put His compassion on me to help hurting people, I really didn't want to do this. You have to know that, when I was young, many people told me the miracles ended when the disciples died. This was a subject I felt uncomfortable with in my Christian walk. His love would come on me so strong, I had to obey Him. God wants to love us so much, until our cup is overflowing! He told me to act on His Word and He would do the rest. He wants us to believe the Bible, over our symptoms, situations, and circumstances. Faith comes from hearing the Word. Romans 10:17 And healing comes through faith in God's promises! 2 Corinthians 1:20 He tells us we can't please Him without faith. Hebrews 11:6 Jesus says over and over in the gospels, your faith has made you whole! Mark 5: 34 Real Faith thrives on a test. Faith lives in the light of anticipated results. Truth supersedes facts, it overrules present circumstances! John 8:31-32 Persistent faith always win! Allow no symptoms to change your attitude toward God's Word! Settle it in your heart that

God's promises will be fulfilled in your life! It may require 7 trips around the walls (Joshua 6:15-16) or 7 dips in the river (2 Kings 5:14) but the victory will come through persistent faith in what God has spoken! Make sure you have a daily Bible reading, and enjoy a life of victorious faith. God always honors His Word! Matthew 17:20 Coach

- This is a prayer in the Bible that I love to share everywhere I go. The Lord bless you and keep you [protect you, guard you, sustain you].The Lord make His face to shine upon you [with favor] and be gracious to you [surrounding you with loving kindness]; May the Lord lift up His countenance [face] upon you [with divine approval], and give you peace [a tranquil heart and life] Numbers 6:24-26 Pray this over your family and friends! Coach

- The twist and turns of life can make it seem like the weight of it is too much to bear. The guilt of yesterday may seem to leave you in a state of despair. But don't lose hope. I want you to know, when you stumble and fall, God's grace covers it all. The Bible says, For I am confident of this very thing, that He who began a good work in you will perfect it until the day of Christ Jesus! Phil. 1:6 Your next chapter will be the greatest of them all. Trust Jesus! Pray for me too! I am going into uncharted waters! Coach

- Did you know that the Lord has supplied us with all the power we need to win the race for Christ. In Acts 1:8-But you will receive power when the Holy Spirit has come upon you, and you will be My witnesses… and to the ends of the earth. This was the last known words of Jesus during His earthly ministry. Then He was taken up into heaven, He sits on the right side of God, and He prays for us.

Acts 1:8 represents the passing of the baton between the Son and the Spirit regarding the divine mission on earth. His physical presence was replaced, so to speak by the Holy Spirit. God wants you to know, He will fill you with the Holy Spirit to carry out His perfect plan in your life! The Holy Spirit is the source of power that will dominate, demonic activity and spiritual darkness on earth! I want you to know, you have all the power you need, to become more than a conqueror through Christ! Romans 8:37 Coach

- God wants to use you to make an impact on this generation, for the gospel. If you will seek the Lord each day, you are exactly who God wants to use for His glory! Even if you feel like you are a failure, second-rate, and inferior, God wants to use you today. God has chosen the weak things of the world to confound the things that are mighty. 1 Corinthians 1:27 God used a puny teenager to take down the biggest giant in the land! God used Paul, who killed Christians, to make the greatest impact in the New Testament! God loves to use nobodies all over the world. The devil fears believers, because he knows the power and authority we possess. If we will walk in the spirit and stay close to Jesus, we will win the battle and see many come to Christ! If you believe in Jesus, you are more than qualified to be a trailblazer for the Lord! Let's roll and help others go to Heaven. Coach

- If you will confess me before people, I will confess you before My Father in Heaven. Matthew 10:32 And I, when lifted up from the earth, I will draw people to Myself. John 12:32 These are two wonderful promises. God spreads the gospel only through human lips. The greatest way to say thank you to God, for the gift of His Son, is to share this incredible message with others. You are a part of the winning team. God will never leave you or forsake you. Hebrews 13:5 Another wonderful promise is found in John 10:28, I give them eternal life, and they will never perish, no one will snatch them out of my hand. This verse will keep you strong and vibrant as you share the love of Jesus. Coach

- I am going to give you an exact way to get back on track, with the Lord. And the amazing blessings that will flow into your life, if you believe these verses in the Bible. It is found in Psalms 103:1-5 Do like David and Praise the Lord with your whole heart each morning. You may have been through a lot of stuff, but you are still alive! Here are the benefits every Christian can enjoy each day!

1) He will forgive all your sins.
2) He will heal all your diseases.
3) He will redeem your life from the pit.
4) He will crown you with His love and compassion.
5) He will satisfy you with amazing things.
6) He will renew your youth like an eagle.

What a great God we serve! Don't forget His benefits for every believer in Christ! Coach

- The Word speaks to us as Jesus would if He were visibly among us. John 1:1,14 The Word has the same authority as He would have if He were to appear among us. The word is always now. It is always fresh and new. It is always the voice of God. The Word is like its author, eternal, unchangeable, and living. Hebrews 4:12 God and His Word are one. The Word is my healing and strength. I can do everything the Bible says I can do! It is the very ability of God in me! Jesus defeated Satan with the Word. And you can do the same thing. Matthew 4:1-11 Dust off your Bible, and open it up, and you will be blessed beyond measure! Coach

- We are in a spiritual battle, and we get to choose each day to be led by the Spirit or to walk in the flesh. Everyone has been bruised, nicked up, and has battle scars but you survived. Some of you feel like you are losing the battle, and others are under the assault from the enemy today. I want you to know, we all a work in progress, none of us are perfect. But I want to encourage you to get back on your horse and continue to fight the good fight of faith! There is a king in you, visions to decree, demons to dominate, and Goliaths to defeat! We will not turn back, and return to living in sin. The Lord says, He will make His face shine upon you! Numbers 6:24-26 We are going to share God's love everywhere we go! We are going to keep encouraging hurting people. Let's put on the whole armor of God and dominate the enemy. Let's roll! Jesus is coming back soon! Coach

- As I was praying today, I felt led to share 2 promises for people who have been waiting patiently for the Lord to answer their prayers. I have heard your prayers and seen your tears. I Will Heal You! 2 Kings 20:5 Also the Lord declares in His Word, If you serve Me, I will take sickness away from your midst. Exodus 23:25 Take the Lord at His Word and you will be healed! Mark 5:34 Coach

- No one can duplicate you. Nobody on earth has your finger print or DNA. You are special. You are one of a kind. You are fearfully and wonderfully made. Psalms 139:14 Millions of years ago, God knew the exact day you would be birthed out of your Mother's womb! The Bible says, His thoughts for you outnumber the sand on the beach! Psalms 139:17-18 God loves you and values you no matter how many mistakes you have made. You are God's Masterpiece! Coach

- Prayer is a powerful tool to strengthen your Christian walk. Prayer is simply pouring your heart out to God. Prayer brings heaven to earth! Prayer can renew, refresh, revive, and restore you. Prayer can make your relationship with God closer than ever. Jesus had to do it! In 1988, I found this verse about prayer and it changed my life! I tell you, whatever you ask for in prayer, believe you have received it, and it will be yours. Mark 11:24 God meant what He said! Praise Him! Coach

- I have never seen so much bickering, turmoil, and hatred going on in our country. The devil is trying to make Christians to retreat and be passive. The Bible says, be strong and courageous, do not be terrified or intimidated, for the Lord your God is with you wherever you go! Joshua 1:9 The Lord, through this administration, has kept the door open for our Christian freedom, and has given us time for a great move of God across the country! If we will seek the Lord and pray, he will hear from heaven and HEAL our land! 2 Chronicles 7:14

In the near future, I really believe you will see 3 amazing things happen! You will see your children and grandchildren be used mightily by the Lord! You will see Roe vs Wade be overturned! You will see Billy Graham type crowds fill stadiums again, wanting to go to heaven! What a great time to be serving the Lord! Jesus defeated Satan on the cross! We win! Let's Roll- Jesus is coming back soon! Coach

- The greatest move you can ever make in your life, is to call on Jesus! He died on an old rugged cross for you! The Bible says: And everyone who calls on the name of the Lord, shall be saved. Acts 2:21 If you think your situation is hopeless-Call on Jesus! If you are afraid- Call on Jesus! If you need to be set free- Call on Jesus! If you feel overwhelmed- Call on Jesus! When you call on Jesus all things are Possible! Matthew 17:20! Coach

- You may be hurting. You may be crying, You may be worried and frustrated tonight. You can depend on God, and you can depend on me to keep praying for you! The Lord is going to bring you through! The Lord is going to touch you. The Lord is going to turn your situation around! He is going to bless you beyond measure! Speak life over your loved ones and friends! Proverbs 18:21 Just watch God change things tonight! You are going to make it! Quit trying to figure everything out! Just take the Lord at His Word! Hebrews 4:12 & Luke 5:5 Coach

- One of my favorite stories in the Bible is found in Mark 2:1-12 Four great guys took their paralyzed friend on a mat to see Jesus. When they arrived, the crowd outside the house was overflowing. Every time you are going to be blessed and get a breakthrough in your life, someone will be in your way. Satan will always tell you to turn around, there is no hope. But these 4 friends would not be denied, they had made their mind up to overcome all barriers! They tore a hole in the roof and lowered the man down to Jesus!

Jesus saw their faith, and forgave the paralytic of his sins and healed him instantly! Everyone was amazed, and said, I have never seen anything like this! Don't give up, and you will be saying the same thing very soon! Coach

- Some people I talk to, don't believe there is a hell, and others think you can get to heaven by doing good works. Both of these thoughts are lies that Satan uses to deceive us. The Bible says, there is none righteous, not even one. Romans 3:10 We all have sinned and come short of the glory of God. Romans 3:23 To go to heaven, you must confess that Jesus is Lord, and believe God raised Him from the dead. Romans 10:8-10 Jesus is the ONLY WAY to heaven! John 14:6 Now about hell. And whoever was not found in the Book of Life was cast into the lake of fire. Revelations 20:15 Choose Jesus, and you will be found in the Book of Life, and you will go to Heaven forever!! Tell everyone that Jesus CAME to seek and save the lost! Luke 19:10 Coach

- You may feel like your world has been shattered. You may have had so called friends walk out on you. I want to say, the Lord has seen every tear you have shed. And God has a perfect plan for you! Jeremiah 29:11 The Bible says, God's eye is on the sparrow, how much more does He care for you! God watches over us 24 hours a day. He never sleeps nor slumbers. Worrying & fretting is not of God. The Lord is my light and my salvation; whom shall I fear? The Lord is the strength of my life; of whom shall I be afraid? Psalms 27:1 Hold on- Stay strong! God's blessings are going to chase you down! Deuteronomy 28:1-14 Coach

- The devil and even people you know will try to define you by your mistakes. Everyone has stumbled. We all mess up. There are faultfinders and gossipers on every street corner. Let me make this crystal clear, Jesus doesn't define you by your mistakes! That is why He died for you! If you have asked Jesus to forgive you, every mistake you have made has been forgiven and forgotten by the Lord you serve! Hebrews 8:12 Keep pressing on, with your head held up high, thanking the Lord for His Amazing Grace! Don't ever let anyone steal your joy! Nehemiah 8:10 Coach

- You don't need to fight your own battles. Revenge is of the world. God says, I will fight all your battles, don't say a word! Exodus 14:14 Keep on smiling, encouraging, and loving others! You stay in the love walk, in the Spirit, and take the high road! Laugh in the middle of the storm! When we put our trust in the Lord, He always blesses us more than we can imagine! Ephesians 3:20 Satan will be mad and you will be glad! Coach

- The Super Bowl is an amazing event. The game creates so much passion and excitement. The atmosphere is incredible. Parties are everywhere! People having a great time. But this game will soon be over. Heaven will be the greatest event of all time though! If you know Jesus, we will celebrate way more than a trillion years, I'm talking about forever! Do you know the Lord? You can ask Jesus, right now into your life! And he will l save you and you will go to heaven forever! It is that simple! Make sure you punch your ticket to Heaven! It is time to get ready, get on board, Jesus is coming back soon! Coach

- Plastic surgery, being popular, or making a lot of money won't fix your insecurities. But devoting time to study the Bible Will! The Bible says: If you put the Word of God first in your life, it will bring Life and Healing to your entire body! What? Are you serious? Yep! God says so in Proverbs 4:20-22 Coach

- Quit comparing yourself to others, who look like they have it all together. You are watching their highlight reel. You can't see what goes on behind the scenes. Everyone has issues, and goes through storms. We all have struggles and have experienced painful situations. But if you Call on Jesus, He will provide a way of escape for you! He will speak to the storm in your life and peace will flood your soul! He will make you lie down in green pastures! He will lead you by the still waters! Psalms 23 Jesus- the sweetest name I know! Coach

- Praise is such a powerful tool to keep you in fellowship with the Lord! When you praise God in the middle of a storm, you confuse the enemy! Joy will replace your despair. Worship will replace your worry! Do it right now! God loves the praises of His People! His presence will make all of your fears disappear! You are still standing. You are still in your right mind. You still have people that love you! You are still alive! Praise Him! Psalms 34:1 Psalms 150:6 Psalms 103:1-5 Coach

- Jesus is more than this world to me. He paid a price for us so we could have eternal life! When I am down, He picks me up! When I am empty, He fills me! When I am confused, He enlightens me! When I am weak, He gives me strength! When I am sick, He makes me well! Jesus is the same yesterday, today, and forever! Hebrews 13:8 What He did in Matthew-Mark-Luke-John, He will certainly do for you! Mark 9:23 Coach

- Sometimes I reflect on how good Jesus has been to me. I just bask in His Amazing grace! He removed my sins as far as the east is from the west! Psalms 103:12 He blots out every sin I have ever committed, and remembers them no more! Isaiah 43:25 He cast all of my sins into the depths of the sea! Micah 7:19 And when I confess my sin, He is faithful to forgive me instantly! 1 John 1:9 There is no condemnation to those who believe in Jesus! Romans 8:1 We are free! I just preached myself happy! I have to Go! Coach

- The final words Jesus spoke on earth were, " But you will receive power when the Holy Spirit comes upon you, and you will be my witnesses..., and to the ends of the earth." Acts 1:8 Do you know when you let the Holy Spirit guide you-you will find total victory! When you are filled with the Holy Spirit, you can see and do things, that are absolutely impossible in the natural! Matthew 17:20 The Lord has given you power to take down every Goliath you come across! Coach

- Does it seem like you take one step forward and two steps back, in your Christian walk? Are your days filled with regrets and shame? I want you to know God has not forgotten you! I want to assure you God will step in and work everything out for your good! Romans 8:28 Forget your yesterdays, and mistakes, and call on Jesus! Phil. 3:13 You keep living, loving, and moving forward! Jesus will strengthen you, so you can say-All Is Well! The sunshine is coming back into your life! This is your new season! Lift your hands and praise Him! Just one touch from Jesus will make you whole! Matthew 14:35-36 Coach

- When you are in a desperate situation, it may be painful, but it may be your greatest blessing! Why? Because you will get out of your comfort zone, and you will do anything to get to Jesus! That is what happen to the man with leprosy in Mark 1:40-42 This man was contagious with the most despicable disease in the land. He saw Jesus and ran to Him and fell down in front of Him, and begging said, "If it is your will, you can heal me." Jesus moved with compassion, touched Him, and said I am willing, be healed! Instantly the leprosy disappeared, and the man was healed! What do you need tonight? Run to Jesus! Coach

- 2 Timothy 3 tells us how bad the times are going to be. Don't you turn back now! As crazy as this world is becoming, stay close to the Lord! Satan is trying to convince every Christian to retreat, lay low, and be lukewarm. There are some Christian leaders and even pastors scared to address the issues in the pulpit that are destroying America! I want you to know, God knows who He can trust to bring the greatest revival in history! He is going to use a bunch of nobodies too!

Quit worrying about public opinion! The Bible says you will be persecuted if you stand up for Him. After what Jesus has done for us on the cross, that is the least we can do! I could type all night, but I have to say this, Isaiah 40:28-31, will become reality, to those who will fight the good fight of faith! You won't be standing in a long line in the Emergency Room! The Lord will give you physical strength like you have never known! Psalms 103:1-5 The greatest time to serve the Lord is right now! Heaven is going to be unbelievable forever!! Coach

- When you confess your sins, God will make your past failures become a stepping stone instead of a stumbling block. That is what happen to David, after he failed miserably in life. He prayed, "Create in me a pure heart, O God, and renew a right spirit in me. Do not cast me from your presence or take your Holy Spirit from me. Restore to me the joy of your salvation and grant me a willing spirit, to sustain me. Psalms 51:10-12 The Lord will hear your prayer, forgive you, and set you free to serve the Lord with boldness! With the Lord, your setback will become your amazing comeback! 1 John 1:9 Coach

- Jesus is on your side. He knew the day you were born. You are the apple of His Eye. He will never stop loving you. He will redeem you. He will make you strong again. He will forgive you. He will put you back together again. He will give you rest. He will give you strength. He will make a way for you. He will put your smile back on your face. He will make you whole. He will make you love your enemies. He will give you unspeakable joy. He will meet all your needs. He will give you an abundant life. He will heal you! He will become your best friend. He will never leave you! Most of all, Jesus gives you eternal life! John 3:16 & Romans 10:8-10 Come back to Jesus! Coach

- Are you living in fear? Do you feel like there is nowhere to turn? Do you feel like dark clouds are all around you? Well I have found a friend His name is Jesus! He is light and in Him there is no darkness! 1 John 1:5 He will break every chain that is wrapped around you. He will give you a new song to sing. He will give you peace that surpasses all understanding. Phil 4:6 He will make your life have purpose again! Jeremiah 29:11 You can try anything, like I did, to make you happy. But-Jesus is the only way! Call on Him! He will Heal You and give you joy unspeakable! John 15:11 & Matthew 4:23 Coach

- Do you need help tonight? The Bible says, look up, all my help comes from the Lord. Are some of you feeling, weary, and thinking of throwing in the towel? Let me give you some good news, the Lord has heard your cry! Help is on the way! Our help comes from the maker of Heaven and earth! Psalms 121:1-2 Faith is thanking the Lord before your blessing comes! You see faith is believing you are going to get your breakthrough before it happens! Hebrews 11:1,6 Trust the Lord! He will always help you overcome obstacles in your life! Jesus Loves You! Coach

- Satan is trying to make you lose heart. The harder you try the worse it gets. I have been there. When you don't spend time in the Bible, life will become so complicated, and your spiritual energy will become nonexistent. The worries and cares of life will dictate your emotional health, and you will feel like you are on an emotional roller coaster. Well, that is not God's will for you! I am going to give you 3 promises God wants to reveal to you tonight! 1) He will always be close to the Brokenhearted and He will SAVE those who are crushed in spirit! Psalms 34:18 2) The Lord is a refuge for the oppressed, a stronghold in times of trouble! Psalms 9:9 3) If you will serve Me tonight, I will take sickness away from your midst! Exodus 23:25 He created you, can you trust God? His Word will never fail, He is watching over it tonight to perform it for you! Jeremiah 1:12 Coach

- Have you been oppressed by the enemy for a long time? The harder you try, the worse it gets. There is like a hole in your soul, you know the Lord, but you are just barely surviving. At night you wish it was morning, and when you wake up you wish it was night. Every menial task overwhelms you. Everything seems too big to think about. Fear continues to grip you and you feel almost paralyzed. I want to speak into your life tonight, because you are coming out of this situation! The Lord is saying, do not let your heart be troubled again! John 14:1-2 He is calling everyone who is weary and heavy-laden, to come to him tonight, and He will give you perfect REST! Matthew 11:28-30 Satan has lied to you long enough! Jesus paid the price for you to have total victory! Everywhere Jesus went He said," FEAR NOT!" You are coming back, filled with God's power this time! Your smile is coming back! Jesus can Fix anyone who has ever been broken! He did it for me, my dad, my sisters, my friends, my family! And He will do it for YOU! Coach

- As times flies by, and as I get older, one thing I do know that someone is going into a crisis, or they are in a crisis, or with Jesus you will be coming out of one. Psalms 34:19 The Lord told me on July 27th, I had only been on Facebook for 6 days, to encourage others. If only one person gets blessed, I know I honored the Lord! He has been so good to me! So here I go tonight, the Lord gave me this Word this morning. Have all your dreams been broken? Do you feel like everything in your life is falling apart. I want you to know that the Lord is a very present HELP in time of trouble! Psalms 46:1 I want to encourage you to be strong and courageous, the Lord will be with you everywhere you go! Joshua 1:9 God will pick you up every time you fall! God will restore you! God is a healer! He healed me! He is a mighty God! He will deliver you! He has seen every tear that has rolled down your face! God is a miracle worker! God will make a way for you to win, again! The Holy Spirit is here right now! Satan thought he had you down for the last count, but Jesus is coming to rescue tonight! Praise Him. Psalms 91:3 Coach

- If you knew without a doubt, Jesus was coming back in one month, would you change anything in your life? We all need to take an inventory of our lives. Would you pray more? Would you read the Bible more? Would you forgive people that hurt you? Would you make sure your family members knew Jesus? Would you tell everybody about the Lord? Would you make up your mind to serve the Lord with all your heart? Would you quit worrying about what people think? Everyone who has become a Christian, should act like Jesus is coming back tonight! Satan and every person that doesn't believe in Jesus will go to hell forever! Revelations 20:15 If you make Jesus your Lord and Savior, you will go to heaven forever! John 3:16 Choose Jesus tonight! Coach

- The Bible says, if you have faith tiny as a mustard seed, you can move any mountain that stands in your way, and nothing shall be impossible all the days of your life! Matthew 17:20 If you can't believe that verse, then I am going to give you one more promise from God's Holy Word! Truly I tell you, if ANYONE says to that mountain, Go throw yourself into the sea, and not doubt in your heart but believe that what you say will happen, it will be done for you! Mark 11:23 These 2 verses have worked for me every time for over 30 years! God meant what He said, and said what He meant! Try His Word tonight, you will overcome any situation! You will be glad, and the devil will be mad! Coach

- The Bible says, cast all your cares on the Lord, for He cares for you. 1 Peter 5:7 The Bible also says, do not be anxious about anything, but in every situation, by prayer and petition, with thanksgiving, present your request to God. Phil. 4:6 These 2 verses teach us that God gives us the power to never worry again! Take your burdens to the Lord and leave them there! Remember this, when you are thankful and have a heart of gratitude to the Lord, you will never have stress in your life! Coach

- God has given us everything we need to live a Godly life. 2 Peter 1:3 And when you realize every precious promise in the Bible can become real in your life! 2 Peter 1:4 The Holy Spirit will help you forgive your enemies. Will help you laugh in the middle of a storm. Will help you to have peace in a crisis. Will help you keep your joy when people talk about you! Greater is He that lives in you than he that lives in the world! 1 John 4:4 Coach

- New Testament 3:16's will Pump You Up Tonight!
  Most people Know one of the greatest verses in the Bible John 3:16- How to be saved and have eternal life! 2 Timothy 3:16- Tells the Power of the Written Word! Luke 3:16- The Baptism of the Holy Spirit! 1 Corinthians 3:16- The Indwelling of the Holy Spirit! Ephesians 3:16- The Holy Spirit Strengthening! 2 Thessalonians 3:16- The Peace of God Colossians 3:16- The Word Working in You! 1 Timothy 3:16- Christ is absolutely amazing! 1 John 3:16- The Power of God's love! Revelations 3:16- The Danger of being lukewarm! Coach

- When you are going through a painful situation, and your strength is gone. You have to encourage yourself, through the Word! This is what I do all the time. I say, God will never leave me! Hebrews 13:5 God will supply all my needs! Phil. 4:19 By His stripes I am healed! Isaiah 53:4-5 I can do all things through Christ! Phil 4:13 I have perfect peace when I keep my mind on the Lord! Isaiah 26:3 I have peace beyond comprehension! Phil. 4:7 I have angels in charge concerning me! Psalms 34:7 With long life He will satisfy me! Psalms 91:16 He will give me the desires of my heart! Psalms 37:4 He will deliver me out of every affliction! Psalms 34:19 He will give me perfect rest! Matthew 11:28-30 I have everlasting life, I am going to live in heaven forever! John 3:16 When I speak the Word over me, the truth sets me free! John 8:31-32 I can pray for others again, and nothing will be impossible in your life! James 5:16 & Matthew 17:20 Encourage yourself today! God said it and I Believe it!! Coach

- Do you know the Lord's phone number? It is Jeremiah 33:3, call Him up! He says, call on Me and I will show you great and mighty things that you don't know! His email address is Mark 9:23. He says if you can believe, all things are possible to him who believes! ALL THINGS! Blue skies are coming back into your life!! Coach

- Jesus wants to be your best friend. Jesus can heal you tonight. You know there is a million miles between God can and God will! The enemy tells us don't go too far out in faith, if you fail you will look like a fool. I want to say this, God will do anything you believe in the Bible! Jeremiah 1:12 When you agree with God's promises you will be walking with God! Trust the Lord tonight and He will do mighty miracles! Matthew 4:23 Coach

- You will never have victory in your life without a battle! Satan is trying to keep everyone on Defeat street! The Lord is bringing you out to Victory Boulevard! Jesus died on a cross for everyone in the whole wide world! John 3:16 If you were the only person on earth, Jesus would have still died for you! Tell everyone what Jesus has done! Our #1 goal should be, telling people how to get to heaven! Jesus will give you power, and strength to have joy every day! Nehemiah 8:10 And the Lord will supply all your needs! Phil. 4:19 Coach

- If you want to be an effective leader, to impact the world for Christ. This is paramount, Private prayer with the Father = Public power to do the works of Jesus! John 14:12 Jesus had to do it-we do too! Coach

- The Word of God is just information, until we use our faith and believe it. When we act on God's Word it becomes revelation into our lives! The verse that change my life was Hebrews 11:6, You can't please God without faith! How do you get faith? By hearing the Word of God! Romans 10:17 How much faith do you need? All you need is faith tiny as a mustard seed, and nothing will be impossible all the days of your life! Matthew 17:20 If you put the Word in your heart and practice it, when the storms of life come you will be totally secure! Matthew 7:24-28 Be a doer of the Word and you will see mighty miracles! James 1:22 Coach

- I am so glad God's love for us is not based on our performance. I am so glad our salvation, so we can have eternal life, is not based on our performance. I am so glad when we believe in Jesus who died for our sins and confess Him, we go to heaven! Romans 10:8-10 I am so glad when we confess our sins, He removes them as far as the east is from the west! Psalms 103:12 I am so glad when we seek the Lord, He fill us with everything we need! Matthew 5:6 I am so glad he gives us power to never worry again! Phil 4:6 I am so glad when we cry out to Him, He hears us, and delivers us from all of our troubles! Psalms 34:17-19 I am so glad He pours His love in us so we can love everyone, even our enemies! Romans 5:5 I am so glad He will renew our strength, so we can soar on wings like eagles! Isaiah 40:28-31 I could type all night what Jesus has done for me! Jesus is my best friend! Satan hates when I reveal this everywhere, I go, Jesus will heal all your physical and emotional problems! Yes, He will! Psalms 103:3, Psalms 107:20, Jeremiah 30:17, 2 Kings 20:5, Matthew 4:23 I AM SO GLAD TONIGHT! Coach

- One thing I have found out in my six decades on this earth, I grow way more in the Lord in desperate situations. When I can't fix a problem in my own strength, I have to totally rely on God to help me! I get up early and seek Him most of the day. But when I am in a comfort zone, all the bills are payed, everything going good, no crisis, and friends are all around me, I sometimes slack off serving God with my whole heart. My point is this, whether everything is going great or going bad in our life, we should be exactly the same in our walk with Christ! I want to be like Paul- I have learned to be content in every single situation! Phil. 4:11 Because we know that God will supply all our needs! Phil. 4:19 Coach

- God has given you the same grace as he gave Paul, who killed Christians. He has given you the same grace as Shadrach, Meshach, and Abednego in the fiery furnace! Daniel 3 The Lord told me you are coming out of the fire! You are not going to smell like smoke! You are not even going to look like what you have been through! The Lord promises to lead you by still waters again! Psalms 23:2 God is refreshing and restoring you, so you can get back on the battle field, and lead people to Jesus! Your setback has created your greatest come back! Satan thought he had you this time. But God stepped in again! Praise Him tonight! Coach

- Jesus is so awesome and He loves to help you each day! I want to share what He did in one day during His earthly ministry! He healed a leper with no hope with His touch! He healed a centurion's servant by just speaking the Word! By the way, Jesus said, He had never seen as much faith by a human being as the centurion had that day! Jesus spoke to a storm while in a boat and a calm came over the whole sea! Then Jesus healed two men that were demon possessed! I call Matthew 8-All in a Day's Work! Jesus is the physical expression of the exact will of God! Quit putting a ceiling on what you think the Lord can do for you! He is still the same! He is still doing the same things every day! Hebrews 13:8 I forgot he healed Peter's mother-in-law too! Coach

- Hold on! The darkest times are just before daybreak! Always remember right before your greatest breakthrough, the enemy bombards our thought life, telling us to give up! The Lord says, let us not grow weary of doing good, for at the proper time we will reap, if we do not give in! Galatians 6:9 God is saying tonight, everything you put your hand to from now on is going to prosper! Psalms 1:3 Don't let anything or anyone ever steal your joy! Nehemiah 8:10 God has got this! Smile & Laugh! Coach

Dear Jesus,

I thank you for loving me even while I was a sinner. I want to thank you for thinking of me while you were hanging on the cross. Jesus, you are my hero, and I thank you for saving me. I thank you for the Word of God that keeps me strong. I thank you for the honor to serve you each day. I thank you for never giving up on me. I want to praise you for your Amazing Grace, that I did not deserve! I want to thank you for being my best friend. I want to thank you for letting me see so many miracles! I want to thank you for preparing a place for all your children with many mansions! I want to thank you when I see you face to face, you will wipe away every tear. I want to thank you that when we get to heaven, we will never have to say good bye! But in the mean time I want to share Your Love everywhere I go! I love you Jesus!

The Best Is Yet to Come,
Coach

54074708R00078

Made in the USA
Columbia, SC
26 March 2019